TEACHING THE CHILD WITH SPECIAL NEEDS

Jeanette Raymond

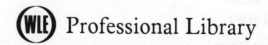 Professional Library

© Jeanette Raymond

First published 1984
by Ward Lock Educational Ltd
47 Marylebone Lane
London W1M 6AX

A Ling Kee Company

ISBN 0 7062 4310 2

British Library Cataloguing in Publication Data

Teaching the child with special needs
1. Exceptional children – Education
I. Title
371. 9   LC3965

ISBN 0 7062 4310 2

Set in 10 on 11 pt Plantin
by GRP Typesetters, Leicester
and printed in Hong Kong

TEACHING THE CHILD WITH SPECIAL NEEDS

Contents

Introduction 1

1 Basic techniques 3
2 Principles of reinforcement 10
3 Recording 12
4 Visual inspection and visual tracking 16
5 Hand–eye co-ordination 21
6 Handwriting 35
7 Communication 45
8 Non-verbal communication 65
9 Cognitive tasks:
  Colour 69
  Number 74
  Telling the time 77
  Concepts and language of time 82
  Concepts of size, weight, length and quantity 87
10 Self-help skills:
  Dressing 100
  Undressing 109
  Encouraging dressing and undressing 111
  Feeding 115
  Toilet training 119
  Brushing teeth 123
11 Skills of independence:
  Domestic skills 124
  Shopping 133
  Using money 135
  Using the telephone 141
  Crossing a road 150
  Using a bus 151
12 Token economy systems 162

References 168

Index 170

To the staff and pupils of Ysgol Ty Coch
whose assistance is gratefully acknowledged

Introduction

The last decade has seen an ever increasing amount of literature on the teaching of children with special educational needs, both of severe and moderate categories (Haring & Schieflebush 1976; Brennan 1974; Blake 1974; Smith 1974; Lerner 1976; Haring & Bateman 1977; Ainscow & Tweddle 1979).*

The 1981 Education Act stated that all children with learning difficulties should be regarded as having special educational needs, whether they attend ordinary schools, or special schools or units. While the Act recognizes that many pupils with special needs will need to be educated in specialist settings, it aims to allow pupils with special needs to be taught in ordinary schools where resources permit, and where the education of mainstream pupils does not suffer as a result. The Act emphasizes that, wherever the teaching takes place, special education should be regarded in terms of quality of teaching and access to resources. This suggests that the expertise required by teachers in special education needs developing in systematic ways so that they can account for the 'special' education they are giving their pupils, and so that good teaching practice will become more widely available to all those who need it.

This book aims to provide a resource for teachers in special education in order that they might approach their work with more definite aims and objectives. It encourages evaluation of teaching programmes with the help of detailed recording schedules and analysis of pupils' responses, so that programmes can be continually modified. Teachers should be able to question not only what they teach, but more importantly, how they teach. In this way they can build up an expertise which will improve the quality of special education in specialist settings. The Warnock Report (1978) suggested that teachers in special education make their knowledge and expertise available to those staff in ordinary schools who may be required to teach pupils with learning difficulties of various kinds. This book should enable teachers in special education to develop valuable knowledge and skills which they could then share with their colleagues in mainstream education. Furthermore, it should enable teachers in ordinary schools to set about developing teaching techniques for special needs pupils, by using the various programmes and record sheets provided.

My aim in writing has been to give concrete examples of how individualized programmes have been constructed for pupils with moderate and severe learning problems. The approach is to analyse tasks into their component parts, to help pupils achieve success in small steps. The results of progress made by individual pupils are included to provide a picture of the length of time the programmes took to complete, the rate of progress and the difficulties experienced by pupils when moving from one step of a programme to the next. In addition, samples of weekly recordings and comments by the teachers carrying out those programmes have been added to provide valuable information and feedback to teachers embarking on similar work.

The examples of specific programmes outlined in this book serve as illustrations for the general text on how to use the concept of *task analysis* to construct programmes. This also involves a discussion on the *objectives approach*, setting criterion levels of success and recording progress in a precise and detailed manner. Most of the available literature discusses techniques without providing actual tried and tested programmes, with results of pupils' progress. Where such programmes are given, they are not graded in small enough steps for pupils with the more severe learning difficulties. There would appear to be a gap in this field which I hope this book goes some way towards filling.

It was impossible to cover every area of development that would be encompassed within a curriculum for children with special needs. A full discussion on this topic can be found in Wilson (1980). The areas I have concentrated on are those with which I have had most requests for help from teachers in special education. The examples of task analysis and the specific programmes should help teachers assess their pupils by using the objectives as a sort of checklist, or as a criterion-referenced test.

Teachers can use the programmes as they are presented or with adaptations to suit the nature of a pupil's need. The various recording methods suggested should enable teachers to choose appropriate ones according to the task in hand. Those samples of record sheets given for children on programmes are the results of two years of trials. They seem to be the most useful for recording the fine detail that is required.

It is hoped that this book will inspire many teachers to develop their own programmes and/or use variations of the many illustrated here. I hope it will also be of help to the teacher with little experience in special education who may feel more able to teach those children with special needs who come within his/her sphere.

*Full details of these and subsequent references are provided on p. 168.

1 Basic Techniques

Task analysis

Breaking down a task into its component parts so that a child with severe learning difficulties can achieve with success is the main aim of task analysis. An E.S.N. (S)* pupil does not learn at the same rate or in the same style as a child in the ordinary school setting. As a result of his/her learning handicap he/she needs more opportunity to practise all the components of a skill or a task in a highly systematic fashion, so that the whole task can finally be executed with a degree of competence. Task analysis aims to increase the child's chances of success by making each step as easy as possible to attain.

The starting and finishing points of a task will vary with the individual, according to his/her maturity, nature of handicap, level of attention, and whether or not a suitable motivator can be found to assist in the learning situation. For instance, a child with a permanent tremor may never achieve complete mastery of a dressing skill. Our final target would then be couched in terms of what the child could achieve with a physical prompt. This type of terminal goal is also known as *successive approximation*. A child with a large uncontrolled tongue may have great difficulty in producing the correct sound with some phonemes, and we would have to accept the best approximation. Some children may not have developed sufficient maturity to be toilet trained and our intermediate goals may have to stop short of the child giving a non-verbal signal of his need.

Task analysis involves analysing areas of the curriculum into tiny steps by writing *behavioural objectives* which describe what the child is expected to do in order to demonstrate mastery of a target. It occasionally also involves us in sequencing the objectives in an order where the performance of one skill necessitates mastery of another skill; for example, a child must be able to grip an object before he/she can place it in a posting box. We must also break a task down in terms of the *conditions* under which we expect the child to execute it, for instance, whether we give the child a verbal clue, whether we model the behaviour prior to the child doing it, whether we hold the child's hand while he/she is doing a task, or whether we simply give an instruction and give no help. We must also set down some *criterion of acceptability*. For some cognitive or language skills, we have to set down some criterion whereby we can assume that the child has 'learned' a skill. For instance, if you are teaching a child to recognize the colour red, then

*The term E.S.N. refers to educational subnormality. E.S.N. (S) indicates severe subnormality, and E.S.N. (M) stands for moderate subnormality.

you may decide that if he/she does it eight to ten times in any one week by pointing correctly when asked to, then you will accept this level of performance, and move on to a new colour. The same principle applies if you are teaching a new word in a sign language or in speech training. Unless you make a decision about *what success means*, then it will not only be soul-destroying for you but damaging to the child's motivation.

Conditions

It is a well known fact that children with severe learning difficulties do not readily transfer their skills from one situation to another, and therefore great care needs to be taken to ensure that *rigidity* does not occur. When specifying conditions under which a behaviour is expected to occur, these must be varied with regard to place, equipment and context in which a skill is taught. For example, if 'money' is always taught using paper coins, a child may fail to transfer the skill to real coins! If a child is taught to count by rote only, he/she may never be able to give you the value of a single digit taken out of its context. Similarly, children can fixate on a particular place in the classroom where a colour is, or on certain objects used to teach a sound, word or colour. It is therefore imperative that part of the programme involves objectives where these factors are varied.

Conditions also refer to the type of help you give a child. Part of your programme may be to take a child through a series of steps with maximum help and ending with minimal or no help. There are five methods that can be used to specify the help given, starting with maximum assistance:

1   Modelling while child attends;
2   Modelling and doing it with child;
3   Giving a physical prompt;
4   Giving a verbal prompt;
5   Giving a verbal instruction.

Modelling refers to demonstrating a task, for example, a sign, an action to be imitated (pointing, drawing, clapping etc.).

A physical prompt may involve simply nudging a child to do a task, or actually taking his/her hand and placing it on a spoon, for example, so that he/she picks it up and completes the feeding process.

A verbal prompt is usually a reminder to the child of what he/she has to do. It can also be part of the child's response which he/she must complete. For instance, if he/she was required to name an object, your prompt may be 'This is a b . . .' for the object 'ball'.

A verbal instruction is simply a command for the child to produce the desired behaviour, for example, 'Finish the jigsaw,' 'Give me the yellow block.'

Writing objectives

An objective is a statement of what a pupil is expected to do in order to demonstrate mastery of a skill. It describes an outcome which can be easily observed and assessed. It provides a very clear indication of exactly what a child is expected to do. As a result it is possible to determine whether or not he/she can do it, and what his/her next target should be.

There is one golden rule to observe when writing objectives, and that is to use a verb (Mager 1975; Gronlund 1978) in the statement. For example, 'Will point to a named colour' is a good objective, whereas 'Knows colours' is a bad objective because there is no indication of how 'knows' is to be interpreted.

Suitable words	*Unsuitable words*
Point	Know
Pick out	Understand
Underline	Appreciate
Say	Enjoy
Sort	Learn
Stack	Achieve
Touch	

Writing objectives means stating the order in which a child will learn a task in a step by step fashion, so that:

1 There is an ongoing record of progress which serves the dual purpose of providing information about where the child is in relation to his/her learning goals, and how far he/she has to go; and also provides a sort of end of term report for parents. Instead of saying 'good', 'satisfactory' or 'slow progress' etc., you can indicate clearly what stage the child has reached in his/her learning.
2 There is continuous feedback about whether your teaching methods are effective or not, and allows immediate adaptation.
3 You know whether your step size is too large or too small.
4 You know the rate at which the child is learning. This is especially important because of the erratic progress often made by children with learning difficulties.
5 Your morale is boosted when you see progress recorded in black and white, and you can see that you are actually getting somewhere!

Sequencing objectives

Most teachers will have learned at teacher training college that children need to go through certain stages of sand and water play, pre-reading exercises etc. in order to attain higher order skills of perception, reading and so on. It may be very tempting therefore to sequence objectives in those terms without having a rationale based on any empirical evidence. It is also easy to fall into the trap of sequencing objectives in a manner that one would expect a normal child to achieve them. We must bear in mind that E.S.N. (S) children and those with specific learning difficulties develop in ways which could mean the achievement of what one would normally consider a more difficult task before a lower order type task, depending on the nature of their handicap. We must also bear in mind that transfer of training from one activity to another cannot readily be assumed, so for instance, finger painting may have no carry over to using a pencil, although you may subsume both tasks under the general heading of 'Perceptual Motor Tasks'.

A useful way of deciding on the sequencing of objectives is presented by Gardner & Tweddle (1979). They suggest that there are three possible 'orders' for analysis of tasks into objectives.

1st order
Here it is assumed that a mastery of one objective is dependent on the mastery of the previous objective, for example:

1 Completes a vertical line of 2 inches.
2 Copies a vertical line of 2 inches.
3 Draws a vertical line of 2 inches.

We would assume that a pupil would find drawing a line easier after he/she has copied it.

2nd order
This is determined by the selected teaching method. Rather than deciding what to teach, we decide on *how* to teach. In general there are four teaching methods used with the severely handicapped. (In many cases similar methods are used with the moderately handicapped pupil.) These are:

A SHAPING   This involves teaching a pupil a particular skill using a variety of different materials which may also vary in size, for example:

Making circular movements on small board with chalk;
Making circular movements on large paper with crayon;
Making circular movements on small paper with crayon;
Making circular movements in book with crayon;
Making circular movements in book with pencil.

B CHAINING   This technique involves breaking a usually flowing action into many small discrete steps. It is best illustrated by looking at self-help skills.

Putting on a dress

Backward chaining:
1 Will pull dress down from hips.
2 Will pull dress down from waist.
3 Will pull dress down from chest.
4 Will pull left sleeve down from elbow.
5 Will pull right sleeve down from elbow.
6 Will pull L/R sleeve down from shoulders.
7 Will put L/R arms into armholes.
8 Will pull dress down from neck.
9 Will pull dress down from head.
10 Will pull dress over head.

Forward chaining:
1 Will pull dress over head.
2 Will pull dress down from head.
3 Will pull dress down to neck.
4 Will put L/R arms into armholes.
5 Will pull L/R sleeve down from shoulders.
6 Will pull L/R sleeves down from elbows.
7 Will pull dress down from chest.
8 Will pull dress down from waist.
9 Will pull dress down from hips.

Backward chaining is usually used with the severely handicapped as their chances of success are greater if they actually begin by completing the task.

C ERRORLESS DISCRIMINATION LEARNING This technique is most useful when teaching a pupil to distinguish items such as colours, numbers, letters, coins etc. It gradually increases the pupil's choice, so that it begins by giving the pupil almost instant success. It is also useful when teaching bliss symbols,* or other symbols on a pointing machine, for example:

1 Will point to the number 1 when asked to do so with no other number present.
2 Will point to the number 1 when asked to do so with the number 3 in array.
3 Will point to the number 1 when asked to do so with the numbers 1 and 3 reversed in position.
4 Will point to the number 1 when asked to do so when the numbers 3 and 9 are present.

*Bliss symbolics is a system of communication taught to children who do not speak. It involves a set of symbols presented on a board, to which children point in an effort to make their communication.

5   Will point to the number 1 when asked to do so, with all the numbers in different orders.
(etc.)

D   FADING   This technique aims to provide maximum visual cues, and gradually remove them. For instance to help a pupil form a letter, number or shape you could outline it with dots, or give colour codes to indicate starting points.

3rd order   At this level, the actual help given in the form of modelling and prompting is included in the programme. See the section on 'Conditions' (p.4) for an explanation of these procedures. There are several examples of this level of analysis in many of the programmes included in this book.

Diagrammatic representation of task analysis

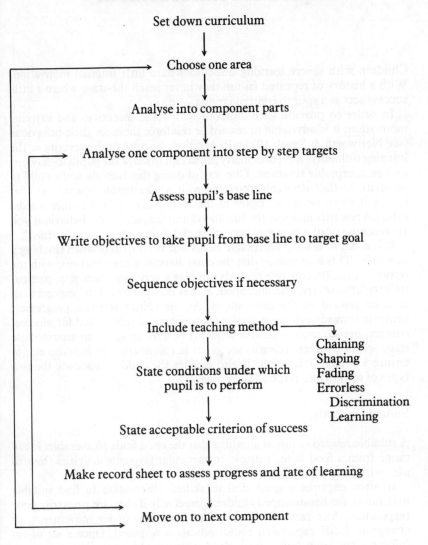

Set down curriculum

↓

Choose one area

↓

Analyse into component parts

↓

Analyse one component into step by step targets

↓

Assess pupil's base line

↓

Write objectives to take pupil from base line to target goal

↓

Sequence objectives if necessary

↓

Include teaching method ————→

Chaining
Shaping
Fading
Errorless
Discrimination
Learning

State conditions under which
pupil is to perform

↓

State acceptable criterion of success

↓

Make record sheet to assess progress and rate of learning

↓

Move on to next component

2   Principles of reinforcement

Children with severe learning difficulties have little internal motivation. With a history of repeated failure they never reach the stage where a little success acts as a spur to continue trying.

In order to provide such children with some incentives and external motivation, it is advisable to reward or reinforce them for their behaviour (see Neisworth & Smith 1973). In addition, because of the severity of the learning difficulty, it is particularly important to *shape* the pupils' behaviour into an acceptable response. One way of doing this is to allow the child to associate his/her desirable response with a pleasurable reward, so that he/she is more likely to engage in that behaviour again. In other words, external rewards increase the likelihood and frequency of a behaviour you are teaching until it becomes part of the child's repertoire, or is 'learned'.

It is usual to reward acceptable behaviour immediately when teaching a new task. This is to ensure that the child associates the behaviour with the reward. Initially, concrete rewards can play a very important role, particularly with the severely handicapped, as they may not be able to respond to an abstract reward in the early stages. As the child's learning progresses, concrete rewards can be gradually withdrawn and substituted for physical contact, praise, smiles etc. It is probably best to engage in an intermediate stage where concrete rewards are given in conjunction with praise etc. to ensure a smooth transition. It also enables the child to associate the two types of reward and respond accordingly.

Suitable rewards

A suitable reward is almost anything that the child finds pleasurable. It can range from a food item, a drink, to particular favourite activities, toys to play with, music, or physical contact.

It often requires a great deal of skilled observation to find suitable motivators for handicapped children, especially if they are primarily poor responders. Any reaction, be it a blink, odd arm or leg movements, or change in facial expression could indicate a response. Once a set of reinforcers has been found for a child, they should be used to maximum advantage. They may often need interchanging so that the child does not tire of them. Some of the reinforcers used are:

Crisps	Playing with textured paper
Sweets	Playing with water
Biscuits	Going on the rocking horse
Tea	Listening to music

Holding hand with adult
Having a cuddle
Smile
Praise and smile
Praise and cuddle

Going for a walk
Watching TV
Sitting near adult
Finger painting

If food or drink is used as a reinforcer then small quantities should be used, for example, one crisp or one sip of a drink. If the reinforcer is physical contact or an activity, such as painting, then it should be for a specified time limit, not more than five minutes approximately.

Tokens

For older children and those who are able to 'delay gratification', a token reward can be given, such as counters, stars, ticks on a chart, or coloured squares. These are collected and exchanged for more concrete rewards at a later stage. As the child receives something immediately, he/she is able to wait to get a more tangible reward. It often has spin-offs in giving counting practice and allows the child some choice in how to spend them. It also provides feedback about their behaviour.

See chapter 12 on 'Token Economy Systems' (p.162) for examples of programmes in this area.

3 Recording

The importance of recording

It is essential that the progress of a pupil be recorded in as detailed a manner as necessary to provide the teacher with the information he/she needs to decide (a) on the suitability of the task selected, (b) whether the steps are graded finely enough, (c) when to move on from one step to the next, (d) whether to skip some steps if it seems that the pupil progresses without the high degree of built-in practice! It is also useful for teachers to compare the rate of progress for their pupils who may be following the same programme. This will indicate which pupils need more time and practice to consolidate learning on certain tasks.

Permanent records of a pupil's progress on a task can show both parents and a new teacher how the pupil learned, how long it took, and the level of success achieved. This is reinforcing for the teacher in two ways. Firstly, it minimizes the subjectivity that creeps into assessments of generalized performance ('did fairly well'; 'not as good today as yesterday') due to the teacher's own mood, expectations and other classroom conditions that are not usually amenable to control. Secondly, because objectives can be written in small step sizes, subtle progress can be measured and provides valuable feedback to the teacher. Progress that is usually erratic and subtle often goes unnoticed and this can be demotivating to the teacher, who may feel that his/her hard work is of little avail, when in fact this may not be so.

Types of record keeping

There are many forms of record keeping and the type to choose will depend on the task and level of learning difficulty experienced by the pupil concerned. In general, the smaller the step size in a programme, the less complicated the recording needs to be. The more complex a task is for a pupil in terms of the number of stages a task has to be broken down into, the more detailed the recording needs to be. The less complex type of programme could use a method of recording whereby the starting and completion date of each step of the programme is recorded, as shown on page 64 for 'Expressive Language'.

The more complex programme involving various degrees of prompting and assistance for the child with more severe difficulties will need more detailed recording. It will be important to know the pupil's responses in three categories:

Successful;
Attempted/unsuccessful;
No response.

Children with severe learning problems can be unpredictable, erratic and inconsistent in their responses. For this reason it is useful to have these categories and to decide on a number of 'trials' per day for every step on a programme. In order to obtain a reasonable estimate of performance taking into account mood and other variables, five trials a day is a handy guide. However, with over-active pupils, or with those who respond minimally, ten trials a day is probably a better guide. The three categories above provide illuminating information. Often pupils are unable to achieve an objective precisely, and therefore recording attempts can show effort, and how closely they are approximating to the target. The steady decrease of 'attempts' and increase in rate of 'successes' can indicate the turning point for the pupil in performing the task to criterion level.

Converting raw data into percentages per category, per week, provides the information about whether the criterion of success has been achieved. Using percentages also enables a teacher to take into account absences by a pupil, school trips or other events which would disrupt the normal pattern of recording. If a pupil only managed twenty trials on a task one week but the full fifty another week, the use of percentages would even out this anomaly. A typical record sheet for this type of recording is shown on page 15.

Often children are able to execute a task, but need some sort of external motivation to perform, and a record of their behaviour needs to be kept. This may simply involve noting whether a child has or has not carried out a task, for example, dressing. By itemizing all the items of clothing, it can be seen quite easily whether (a) the child dresses completely or partially and (b) which articles of clothing are proving difficult for the child. An example of this type of chart is given on page 114 in connection with monitoring a pupil's perseverance in dressing and undressing herself. Similarly, with behaviours like toilet training a record needs to be kept of how often a pupil is wet, dry or soiled, and/or uses a pot. This type of record is often called a *frequency chart*. Such a chart would involve breaking up a day into equal periods of time, for example, half hour, quarter hour or hourly intervals to note down the frequency of a particular behaviour. An example of this type of record sheet is shown on page 122 for 'Rapid Toilet Training'.

It may sometimes be necessary to record behaviour which is 'disturbing' to teachers, parents or peers. This is particularly so if such behaviours are seen to be preventing the pupil achieve the goals set for him/her. For instance, pupils who are highly distractible, scream or shout, or indulge in self-mutilation, as well as those who are very active with short attention spans will disrupt their learning progress. Before specific educational/social goals can be set for them and implemented, these disturbing behaviours need to be reduced. Sometimes the child being occupied on a task is enough to reduce the undesirable behaviour. Other times this is not so, and a dual approach needs to be taken. Both the behaviour in question and the child's performance on a task need to be simultaneously recorded. This is called a *baseline recording* to enable a teacher to get accurate information about the frequency and time of occurrence. A simple way of doing this would be to measure 'on task' behaviour, i.e. when a pupil was doing a specified activity, and whether he/she also screamed, talked, threw things etc. depending on the behaviour in question.

Baseline record of on task behaviour and screaming

KEY √ = on task   x = off task   · = scream

Time a.m.	Mon.	Tues.	Wed.	Thurs.	Fri.
9.15 – 9.30	√	√ ·	x · · ·	√	√
9.30 – 9.45	√	√	x · · ·	√	√
9.45 – 10.00	√ ·	x · ·	√	√	√
10.00 – 10.15	x · ·	x · · · · ·	√	√	√
10.15 – 10.30	x · · ·	√	√	x	√
10.30 – 10.45	x · · ·	x · ·	x	x ·	√
10.45 – 11.00	√	x	x · ·	√	x
11.00 – 11.15	√	x ·	x ·	√	x · · · ·
11.15 – 11.45	√	x	x · · · ·	x	x ·
11.45 – 12.00	√ · ·	x · · ·	x · · · ·	x ·	x ·

Total on task =	7	3	3	6	6
Total screams =	11	14	17	2	6

From the above record a pattern can be detected. The pupil is more likely to scream when 'off task' and appears to be off task more during the second half of the morning. A plan of action could then be drawn up as to whether tasks need changing *per se*, whether they are given for too long a period, whether the pupil needs more help in doing them etc. Records could then show whether the changes implemented have been effective, by comparing the child's behaviour with the baseline measurement.

More detailed accounts of measuring and controlling behaviour can be found in Neisworth & Smith (1973); Krumboltz & Krumboltz (1972); Poteet (1976); Blackham & Silberman (1975); Gardner (1972); and Kiernan

& Woodford (1975). Presland (1981) gives an excellent review of behaviour
modification in special schools with severely handicapped pupils.

Sample record sheet

Name: J.D.   *Criterion of success:* 75%
Task: Scribbling   *Week number:* 1
Step: Will make horizontal
movements with a crayon when
teacher's hand guides her.

KEY
√ = completed/successful
o = attempted/unsuccessful
x = no response

Totals

Trials	Mon.	Tues.	Wed.	Thurs.	Fri.	Success	Attempt	No resp.
1								
2								
3								
4								
5								
6								
7								
8								
9								
10								
				Grand totals				

Percentages
successful =
attempted/unsuccessful =
no response =

4 Visual inspection and visual tracking

Many severely handicapped pupils, especially those in the special care sections of special schools, need to be trained in the skills of visual inspection and tracking of objects in their visual fields if they are to become aware of people and objects around them, and interact with them. Kiernan *et al.* (1978) break these abilities down into stages. They include looking at one object, looking from one object to another, following a moving object with the eyes, and combining vision and touch. Kiernan & Jones (1977) provide a detailed assessment guide which can be used to decide what the child can do and where to begin a teaching programme.

Looking at one object

Techniques
Prompting
Fading
Shaping

Objects
Dark card type paper
Shiny object – silver paper, ring
Toy which emits sound
Toy which changes in appearance, e.g. face of a clown doll
Picture book
Bag of textured materials – foam, cork, towel, wool, stone
Magnetic board with shapes/familiar magnetic objects
Bouncing/moving toy
Model race track with cars/trains
Roly-poly toy
Toy held by string
Yo-yo
Torch

Objectives (3rd order analysis)
1 Will look at shiny paper/ring held up against dark card when teacher holds child's head upright towards shiny object for three seconds, verbally describing object.
2 Will look at shiny paper/ring when held up against dark card, when teacher holds child's head upright towards shiny object for five seconds, verbally describing the object.
3 As above when shiny object is at 60° angle to the left.
4 As above when shiny object is at 60° angle to the right.

5   Will look at shiny paper/ring held up against dark card when teacher gives a physical prompt, pointing to the object and describing it verbally.

6   As above when shiny object is at 60° angle to the left.

7   As above when shiny object is at 60° angle to the right.

8   Will look for five seconds at shiny object held up against dark card when teacher points to the object giving verbal prompt.

9   As above when shiny object is at 60° angle to the left.

10   As above when shiny object is at 60° angle to the right.

11   Will look at large object emitting a sound, e.g. a squeezy toy, when given a physical prompt.

12   As above with a verbal prompt.

13   As above turning head to the right when teacher helps pupil to turn head.

14   As above turning head to the left when teacher helps to turn head.

15   Will look at it and smile when toy emitting sound is placed in front of pupil, with a physical prompt.

16   As above with a verbal prompt.

17   As above when toy emitting sound is placed in various fields of vision, including the up, down, and sideways positions.

18   Will reach out for face-changing clown toy when placed in front of pupil, with a physical prompt.

19   As above with verbal prompt.

20   Will hold face-changing clown when placed in preferred hand, and look at the face while teacher is manipulating expression on clown's face.

21   As above with a verbal prompt.

22   Will reach out for clown (smiling) when placed immediately in front of pupil, given a physical prompt.

23   As above with a verbal prompt.

24   Will try to manipulate expression on clown's face, while looking at the toy, with a physical prompt.

25   As above with a verbal prompt.

26   Will place preferred hand in a bag of textured materials when teacher holds pupil's hand, and bring out a piece of foam, looking at it and smiling.

27   Will manipulate piece of foam in both hands with physical guidance from teacher.

28   As above with verbal prompting.

29   Will place preferred hand in bag of textured material when teacher holds pupil's hand, and bring out the cork manipulating it with the thumb and two fingers, with physical guidance.

30   As above but moving the cork from one hand to another.

31   As above with a physical prompt.

32   As above with a verbal prompt.

33   Repeat for all other material in texture bag.

Looking from one object to another

Objectives (3rd order analysis)

1   Will look at a picture book of a familiar object, and then turn head to look at large toy introduced to left visual field when teacher holds pupil's head and directs it to new object.
2   As above with a physical prompt, when new object is described verbally.
3   As above with a verbal prompt.
4   As above but in the right visual field.
5   Will divert gaze from a small toy in immediate field of vision to a large object brought into visual field, with physical guidance.
6   As above with verbal prompting.
7   Will divert gaze from a small object in visual field to another, noise-making object introduced into the same visual field, with verbal prompting.
8   Will divert gaze from a small object in left and right visual fields to another, noise-making object, with verbal prompting.
9   Will divert gaze from shape/object in front of pupil on a magnetic board when another shape/object is placed near the first object, with physical prompting.
10 Will reach out and touch second object on magnetic board when physically guided.
11 Will move second object on magnetic board with physical guidance.
12 Will move second object on magnetic board when given a verbal prompt.
13 Will look at large object placed in upper right hand corner of magnetic board, with physical guidance.
14 Will move object placed in upper right hand corner of magnetic board, with physical prompting.
15 As above with verbal prompt.
16 Will look at large object placed in upper left hand corner of magnetic board, with physical guidance.
17 Will move object placed in upper left hand corner of magnetic board, with physical guidance.
18 As above with verbal prompting.
19 As for objectives 13, 14, and 15, with objects placed in lower right and lower left hand corners of magnetic board.
20 Will watch bouncing toy on a table with physical guidance, and then divert gaze when a noisy large toy is placed on the table.
21 As above with physical prompt, e.g. pointing to new toy.

Following moving objects with the eyes

Objectives (3rd order analysis)
1 Will follow track of shiny object on dark paper when teacher holds child's head and directs gaze.
2 As above with slight physical prompting, pointing to the shiny object as it moves.
3 As above with verbal prompting.
4 Will follow a toy, e.g. car moving along the table when teacher holds child's head and directs his/her gaze.
5 As above with slight physical prompting.
6 As above with verbal prompting.
7 Will follow a car/train on a track with physical guidance.
8 As above with verbal prompting.
9 Will follow a toy dropped from table height to the floor, with physical guidance.
10 As above with slight physical prompt, e.g. pointing.
11 As above with a verbal prompt.
12 Will watch toy rolling from one side of the table to another, with physical guidance.
13 Will watch toy rolling from one side of the table to another, with physical prompt.
14 As above with verbal prompting.
15 Will watch adult's face moving from left to right in pupil's field of vision, when physically directed.
16 As above with physical prompt.
17 As above with verbal prompt.
18 Will watch yo-yo being manipulated up and down, when being physically directed.
19 As above with physical prompt.
20 As above with verbal prompt.

Combining vision and touch

Some objectives incorporate this skill in the sections on looking at one object, and looking from one object to another, but the category is treated as a separate entity here for the purposes of clarity.

Objectives (3rd order analysis)
1 Will hold teacher's hand and move a car on a table.
2 Will move a car on a table given a physical prompt, following the car with his/her eyes.
3 As above with a verbal prompt.
4 Will hold teacher's hand and move a toy held by a string.
5 Will move a toy held by string with a physical prompt following the progression of the toy with his/her eyes.

6   Will move parts of a body placed on a magnetic board given a physical prompt.

7   As above with a verbal prompt.

8   Will hold teacher's hand on torch and make a moving light shine on the dark card-type paper.

9   Will make own moving light on dark paper with torch when given a physical prompt.

10   As above with verbal prompt.

11   Will move two cars on a table watching them, with physical guidance.

12   As above with verbal guidance.

13   Will try to cover stone with shiny paper when given physical guidance and demonstration.

14   As above with physical prompting.

15   As above with verbal prompting.

16   Will reach for toys that make noises when placed on the table and attempt to obtain sounds, with physical prompting.

17   As above with verbal prompting.

18   Will attempt to tie wool around fingers with physical guidance.

19   As above with physical prompt.

20   As above with verbal prompt.

The programmes suggested above cannot be carried out effectively without continuous reinforcement. This needs to be given instantly, and usually in the form of physical affection, smiles, and praise. Such physical contact should also have the benefit of encouraging pupils to reach out for objects and people themselves.

5 Hand–eye co-ordination

The following five programmes were constructed for a young seven-year-old, hyperactive pupil, J.D., with no speech. She had a mental age of eighteen months. She did 'scream' frequently, but the screams were distinguishable in terms of pleasure, anger, frustration etc. As a result of her hyperactivity she was unable to sit down and concentrate on tasks, and needed very finely broken down steps to be seen to be achieving anything. Hand–eye tasks were chosen so as to help J.D. to sit for increasing periods of time, to develop an attention span of more than ten seconds, which was her baseline measurement.

Tasks were analysed for her in the following manner:

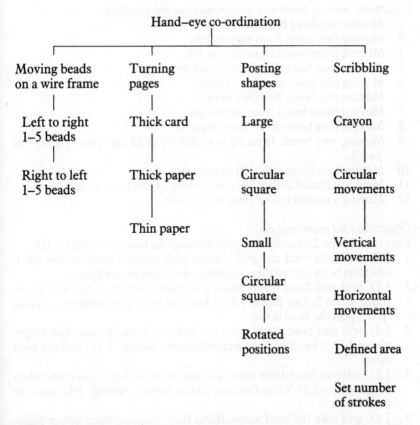

The programmes were carried out in the morning session of the school day. She was given ten trials on every step of each programme, so as to obtain a reasonable estimate of performance. An overall criterion of 75 per cent success per step was set.

1   Moving beads on a wire frame
2   Scribbling
3   Turning pages of a book
4   Posting shapes
5   Inset board

Techniques
Shaping
Backward chaining
Prompting
Fading

Objectives: moving beads on a wire frame (2nd order analysis)
1   Moving one bead from right to left.
2   Moving two beads from right to left.
3   Moving three beads from right to left.
4   Moving four beads from right to left etc.
5   Moving one bead from left to right.
6   Moving two beads from left to right.
7   Moving three beads from left to right.
8   Moving four beads from left to right etc.
9   Moving two beads from right to left (if child can grasp concept of 'two').
10   Moving two beads from left to right etc.
11   Moving a named colour from left to right (if child can identify colour).
12   Moving a named colour from right to left.

Objectives (3rd order analysis)
For: step 1 from 2nd order analysis: Moving one bead from right to left.
1   J.D. will grip bead and pull it down with helper's hand on hers when bead has been moved three-quarters of the way across frame.
2   J.D. will pull bead down when it is three-quarters of the way across frame when helper places J.D.'s hand on bead and withdraws, saying 'J.D., pull the bead down.'
3   J.D. will pull bead down when it is half-way across frame when helper places J.D.'s hand on bead and withdraws, saying, 'J.D., pull the bead down.'
4   J.D. will pull bead down when it is quarter of the way across frame when helper places J.D.'s hand on bead and withdraws, saying, 'J.D., pull the bead down.'
5   J.D. will take the bead across frame from the start when helper places J.D.'s hand on bead and says, 'J.D., take this bead to the other side.'

This analysis can be carried out for the remaining 2nd order analysis as required. Fig. 1 gives in chart form the results of J.D.'s progress after seventeen weeks. The steps of the programme are shown under the horizontal axis.

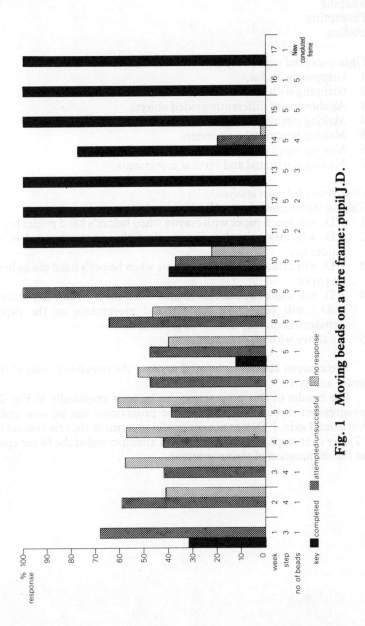

Fig. 1 Moving beads on a wire frame: pupil J.D.

Scribbling – Programme 1

Techniques
Modelling
Shaping
Prompting
Fading

Objectives (2nd order analysis)
1 Gripping with fist.
2 Gripping with thumb and index finger.
3 As above with differently graded objects.
4 Making circular movements.
5 Making horizontal movements.
6 Making vertical movements.
7 Making horizontal and vertical movements.

Objectives (3rd order analysis)
Taking step 4 from above: Making circular movements.
1 J.D. will touch paper with crayon when helper's hand guides her.
2 J.D. will make circular movements with crayon when helper's hand guides her.
3 J.D. will make circular movements when helper's hand places her hand on paper.
4 J.D. will make circular movements when she is given a crayon and told, 'J.D., will you make some round movements on the paper.' A demonstration may need to be given first.
5 As above without demonstration.

The analysis above can be used to cover the remaining items of the 2nd order analysis.

The results of this programme can be seen graphically in Fig. 2. The progression through the steps of the programme can be seen under the horizontal axis. J.D. was not successful in terms of the criterion set for her (75 per cent step), although her rate of attempts was at the 84 per cent level at the termination of the programme.

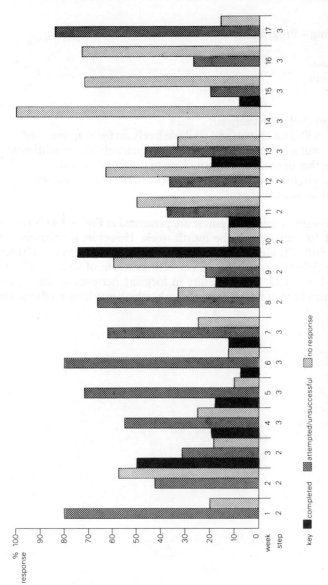

Fig. 2 Scribbling (Programme 1): pupil J.D.

Another programme within the Scribbling framework was constructed for J.D., this time to encourage free movements of crayon/pencil on paper, eventually to restrict this to a certain area on a piece of paper.

Scribbling – Programme 2

Techniques
Prompting
Fading

Objectives (3rd order analysis)
1   J.D. will hold crayon and scribble freely on foolscap size card.
2   J.D. will scribble freely inside a 6 in. square of card (of a different colour from that of the foolscap) stuck on to the foolscap card.
3   J.D. will make at least five vertical or horizontal strokes with crayon on the 6 in. square of card.

The results of this programme are presented in Fig. 3. J.D.'s success rate reached 100 per cent in the fourth week. However, moving on to step 2 proved difficult. Her level of attempts remained high, often at 100 per cent, but she failed to reach the 75 per cent criterion of success. Her teacher reported that J.D. had difficulty in focusing her eyes on the paper. J.D. would turn her head away from the task, which may have produced the poor results.

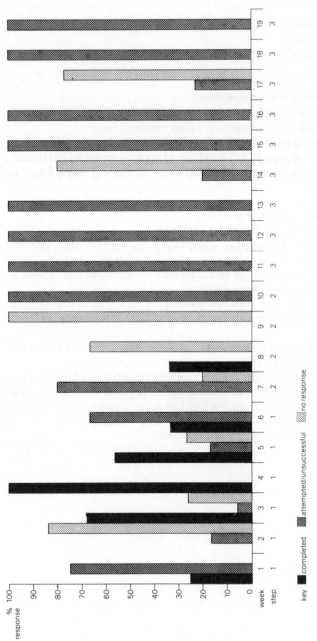

Fig. 3 Scribbling (Programme 2): pupil J.D.

Turning pages of a book

Techniques
Modelling
Prompting
Shaping

Objectives (2nd order analysis)
1   Flicking thick card type pages.
2   Flicking thick pages on a large made up book.
3   Placing page on left side of book when helper has turned page a little.
4   Placing page on left hand side of book when helper has turned it ½–1 in.
5   Getting corner of page between thumb and index finger and turning page.

Objectives (3rd order analysis)
Taking step 3 of 2nd order analysis:
1   J.D. will grip page and place it flat on left hand side of book with helper's hand on hers.
2   J.D. will grip page and place it flat on left hand side of book when helper places J.D.'s hand on page.
3   J.D. will grip page and place it flat on left hand side of book when told 'J.D., put the page down.'

The above analysis can be carried out for steps 4 and 5 on the 2nd order analysis if required.

The results of this programme are presented graphically in Fig. 4. It took J.D. sixteen weeks to achieve the 75 per cent success rate in a consistent fashion. Although she reached 100 per cent success rate at week eleven, she failed to maintain that for the next four weeks. Subsequently she achieved 100 per cent and continued to do so.

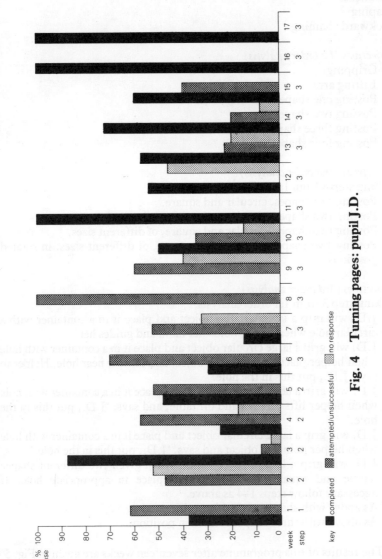

Fig. 4 Turning pages: pupil J.D.

Posting shapes

Techniques
Shaping
Backward chaining

Objectives (1st order analysis)
1   Gripping.
2   Lifting arm.
3   Posting one shape.
4   Posting two shapes.
5   Posting three shapes.
6   Posting four shapes etc.

Objectives (2nd order analysis)
Taking step 4 from 1st order analysis:
1   Posting two shapes, circular and square.
2   Posting two shapes, circular and square, in rotated position.
3   Posting two shapes, circular and square, of different sizes.
4   Posting two shapes, circular and square, of different sizes, in rotated positions.

Objectives (3rd order analysis)
Taking step 3 from 1st order analysis:
1   J.D. will grip a large circular object and place it in a container with a circular hole when helper holds her hand and guides her.
2   J.D. will grip a large circular object and place it in a container with hole when helper places her hand on object and takes it near hole. Helper to say, 'J.D., put this in the hole.'
3   J.D. will grip a large circular object and place it in a container with hole when helper lifts J.D.'s hand off table, and says, 'J.D., put this in the hole.'
4   J.D. will grip a large circular object and place it in a container with hole when helper points to object and says, 'J.D., put this in the hole.'
5   J.D. will grip a large circular object when given two different shapes (circle and square, both large) and place in appropriate hole. If necessary follow steps 1–4 as above.
6   As above with shapes rotated in position.
7   As above with three shapes rotated in position.

The results of this programme after seventeen weeks are given in Fig. 5 It took eleven weeks for J.D. to achieve the required level of success in posting the 'circle', but she achieved much faster success with the next shape of a 'square'.

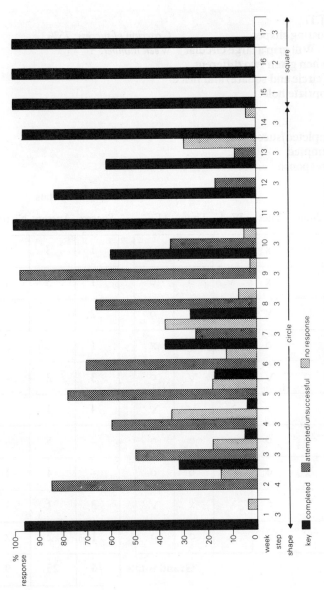

Fig. 5 Shapes – posting shapes: pupil J.D.

Record sheet

Name: J.D.
Task: Posting shapes   *Criterion of success:* 75%
Step: 5   Will grip a large circular   *Week number:* 3
object when given two different
shapes (circle and square) and place
in appropriate hole.

KEY
$\sqrt{}$ = completed/successful
o = attempted
x = no response

Trials	Mon.	Tues.	Wed.	Thurs.	Fri.	Success	Attempt	No resp.
1	o	x	o	o	$\sqrt{}$	1	3	1
2	o	x	$\sqrt{}$	o	o	1	3	1
3	$\sqrt{}$	x	o	$\sqrt{}$	o	2	2	1
4	x	o	o	$\sqrt{}$	x	1	2	2
5	o	$\sqrt{}$	$\sqrt{}$	$\sqrt{}$	o	3	2	–
6	o	$\sqrt{}$	$\sqrt{}$	$\sqrt{}$	$\sqrt{}$	4	1	–
7	o	o	o	o	o	–	5	–
8	x	o	o	o	o	–	4	1
9	$\sqrt{}$	o	$\sqrt{}$	x	$\sqrt{}$	3	1	1
10	$\sqrt{}$	x	x	o	o	1	2	2
Grand totals						16	25	9

Totals (Success, Attempt, No resp.)

Percentages
completed/successful = 32%
attempted/successful = 50%
no response = 18%

The next part of J.D.'s programme involved moving on to an inset board with a square and circle.

Inset board

Techniques
Backward chaining
Shaping
Prompting
Fading

Objectives (3rd order analysis)
1 J.D. will place the square in an inset board when the circle is already in place.
2 J.D. will place circle in inset board when the square is already in place.
3 J.D. will place the circle and the square in inset board when each item is placed by its correct position.
4 J.D. will place the circle and the square in inset board when handed each piece with no physical cues.

Results after nineteen weeks are presented in Fig. 6. J.D. had not achieved 75 per cent success rate on step 4 by the nineteenth week, but was showing a likelihood of success at that level given more time.

Teacher's comments
J.D.'s teacher commented favourably in the main at the end of the period for which the programmes were being operated. She said that she was able to be positive in her approach, and more precise in her aims and methods of teaching. She also felt that having such structured and detailed objectives forced her to actually teach J.D. as opposed to merely contain her as had been the case previously. She actually felt she was achieving something tangible because it was being recorded. It is noteworthy that she mentioned the fact that most teachers recorded what *they* did as opposed to what progress the child had made, and it was the latter that she found most rewarding. The success of being able to do something useful with J.D. reinforced the teacher and nursery assistants, which in turn made them praise her and give her more attention than previously. The finely graded objectives specifying the exact amount and nature of guidance given to J.D. meant that there was little dispute as to whether she had attempted or actually completed the task. This was a great boon for the teacher and nursery nurse as they could be equally consistent in their recordings.

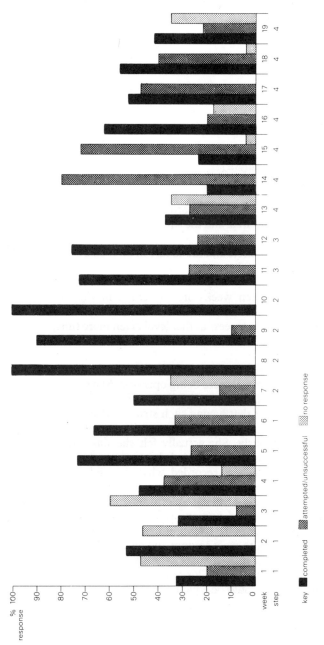

Fig. 6   Inset jigsaws: pupil J.D.

6 Handwriting

Techniques
Shaping
Fading
Backward chaining

Objectives (1st order analysis)
1 Gripping a pencil.
2 Correct pencil hold.
3 Pencil control.
4 Discrimination of large shapes.
5 Discrimination of letters/symbols.
6 Copying letters.
7 Copying words.
8 Writing words spontaneously.

Objectives (2nd order analysis)
A GRIPPING A PENCIL
1 Will hold pencil in preferred hand using a fist hold.
2 Will hold pencil using thumb and forefinger.

B CORRECT PENCIL HOLD: USING SHAPING
1 Will hold pencil approximately one inch from tip, using thumb and forefinger with third finger as support.
2 Will hold pencil ½–1 in. as above, so as to apply pressure on paper.
3 Will hold pencil ½–1 in. as above, with a fluid wrist movement.
4 Will hold pencil ½–1 in. as above, with wrist and arm on the bottom of the paper/desk, so as to maximize feedback.

C PENCIL CONTROL: USING SHAPING
1 Scribbles using crayon.
2 Makes vertical marks using crayon.
3 Makes horizontal marks using crayon.
4 Makes circular marks using crayon.
5 Scribbles using pencil.
6 Makes vertical marks using pencil.
7 Makes horizontal marks using pencil.
8 Makes circular marks using pencil.
9 Draws a line of 4 in. between two lines 1 in. apart without touching the boundary lines.
10 As above in between two lines ½ in. apart.

11 As above in between two lines ¼ in. apart.
12 Draws a line of 2 in. in between two lines 1 in. apart without touching the boundary lines.
13 As above in between two lines ½ in. apart.
14 As above in between two lines ¼ in. apart.
15 Draws a line of 3 in. in between 2 lines 1 in. apart without touching the boundary lines.
16 As above in between two lines ½ in. apart.
17 As above in between two lines ¼ in. apart.
18 Traces four-sided shapes of 3 in. in length.
19 Traces four-sided shapes of 2 in. in length.
20 Traces four-sided shapes of 1 in. in length.
21 Traces three-sided shapes of 3 in. in length.
22 Traces three-sided shapes of 2 in. in length.
23 Traces three-sided shapes of 1 in. in length.
24 Traces two-sided shapes of 3 in. in length.
25 Traces two-sided shapes of 2 in. in length.
26 Traces two-sided shapes of 1 in. in length.
27 Copies circle of 3 in. in diameter.
28 Copies circle of 2 in. in diameter.
29 Copies circle of 1 in. in diameter.
30 Copies square of 3 in. in diameter.
31 Copies square of 2 in. in diameter.
32 Copies square of 1 in. in diameter.
33 Copies triangle of 3 in. in diameter.
34 Copies triangle of 2 in. in diameter.
35 Copies triangle of 1 in. in diameter.

D   VISUAL DISCRIMINATION OF LARGE SHAPES: USING SHAPING
 1   Given large circle can match it with another circle of similar size.
 2   Given large circle can match it with a circle of a different size.
 3   Can point to two circles which are alike in an array of three shapes, where one is different.
 4   Can do above with four shapes where two are different.
 5   Can match squares of equal size.
 6   Can match squares of unequal size.
 7   Can point to two squares in an array of three shapes, where one is different.
 8   Can do above with four shapes where two are different.
 9   Can match triangles of equal size.
10   Can match triangles of unequal size.
11   Can point to two triangles in an array of three shapes where one is different.
12   Can do above with four shapes where two are different.

E   VISUAL DISCRIMINATION OF LETTERS: USING SHAPING
 1   Will match two cards with the same letter on them, in the same colour

and size.
2   Will match two cards with the same letter on them, in the same size but different colours.
3   Will match two cards with the same letter in different sizes and colours.
4   Will pick out a letter in an array of two different looking letters when asked to 'find one like this'.

a / s t a

5   Will do as above with target letter in different positions.

a / a s t

a / s a t

6   Will point to a letter similar to two others in an array when asked to 'find one like this'.

V / V W X

7   Will point to a letter similar to two others in an array with target letter in different positions.

V / W V X

V / X W V

F   COPYING LETTERS: USING FADING AND BACKWARD CHAINING
1   Will trace over an upper case letter formed by teacher.
2   Will 'draw' over an upper case letter formed by teacher.
3   Will complete progressively larger sections of an upper case letter formed by teacher.
4   Will copy an upper case letter with visual cues to indicate starting and finishing points.
5   Will copy an upper case letter with no help.
6   Will trace over a lower case letter.
7   Will draw over a lower case letter.
8   Will complete progressively larger sections of a lower case letter.
9   Will copy a lower case letter with visual cues to indicate starting and finishing points.
10   Will copy a lower case letter with no help.

G   COPYING A WORD: USING SHAPING
1   Will copy a row of identical single letters.
2   Will copy a row of dissimilar letters.
3   Will copy a one-syllable word.
4   Will copy a two-syllable word.
5   Will copy own name.

Let us suppose that your long term aim within the framework of handwriting is to teach a child to write his/her name. The task could be analysed in the following manner:

Suggested task analysis

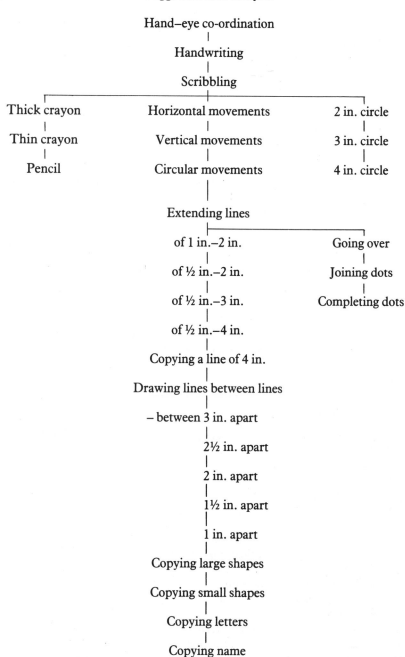

Hand–eye co-ordination
|
Handwriting
|
Scribbling

Thick crayon	Horizontal movements	2 in. circle
Thin crayon	Vertical movements	3 in. circle
Pencil	Circular movements	4 in. circle

Extending lines

of 1 in.–2 in.	Going over
of ½ in.–2 in.	Joining dots
of ½ in.–3 in.	Completing dots

of ½ in.–4 in.
|
Copying a line of 4 in.
|
Drawing lines between lines
|
– between 3 in. apart
|
2½ in. apart
|
2 in. apart
|
1½ in. apart
|
1 in. apart
|
Copying large shapes
|
Copying small shapes
|
Copying letters
|
Copying name

Taking scribbling, extending lines, drawing lines between lines, copying shapes, copying letters, and finally, copying a child's own name, here is the appropriate third order analysis for pupils who will require a maximum amount of guidance and built-in reinforcement.

Scribbling

Techniques
Modelling
Physical ⎱
Verbal ⎰ prompts

Objectives
1 Will hold thick crayon in right fist and make horizontal movements of approximately 2 in. on paper within a circle of 2 in. radius when teacher holds child's hand and models.
2 Will hold thick crayon in right fist and make horizontal movements of approximately 2 in. on paper within a circle of 2 in. radius when teacher takes child's hand to paper.
3 Will hold thick crayon in right fist and make horizontal movement of approximately 2 in. when teacher gives child the crayon and says, 'Mark in the circle.'
4 Will hold thin crayon using thumb and forefinger, and make horizontal movements of approximately 2 in. on paper within a circle of 2 in. radius when teacher takes child's hand and places it on paper.
5 Will hold thin crayon, using thumb and forefinger, and make horizontal movements of approximately 2 in. on paper within a circle of 2 in. radius when teacher gives child the crayon and says, 'Mark in the circle.'
6 Will hold pencil, using thumb and forefinger, and make horizontal movements of approximately 2 in. within a circle of 2 in. radius when teacher takes child's hand and places it on paper.
7 Will hold pencil, using thumb and forefinger, and make horizontal movements of approximately 2 in. within a circle of 2 in. radius when teacher says, 'Mark in the circle.'

The next stage can either be to do as above with vertical lines, or to move on to a 3 in., and then on to a 4 in. radius circle. Whichever is chosen, steps 1–3 need to be repeated with the appropriate wording. It is advisable to write out each step as shown above whichever direction is taken, so that recording is precise.

Extending lines

Techniques
Prompting

Fading
Modelling

Objectives

1 Will hold pencil and go over a horizontal line of 2 in. when teacher holds child's hand and does it with him/her.
2 Will go over a horizontal line of 2 in. when teacher takes child's hand and places it on the left hand side of the line.
3 Will go over a horizontal line of 2 in. when teacher gives child a pencil and says, 'Go over that line.'
4 Will go over a horizontal line of 3 in. when teacher holds child's hand and goes over the line with him/her.
5 Will go over a horizontal line of 3 in. when teacher takes child's hand and places it on the left hand side of the line.
6 Will go over a horizontal line of 3 in. when teacher gives child a pencil and says, 'Go over that line.'
7 Will join dots of ½ in. spaced horizontally to complete a horizontal line of 3 in. when teacher holds his/her hand and does it with him/her.
8 Will join dots of ½ in. spaced horizontally to complete a horizontal line of 3 in. when teacher takes child's hand to the point where dots commence.
9 Will join dots of ½ in. spaced horizontally to complete a line of 3 in. when teacher says, 'Join the dots.'
10 Will complete a line of horizontal dots of 3 in. when teacher holds child's hand and does it with him/her.
11 Will complete a line of horizontal dots of 3 in. when teacher takes child's hand to left hand side of dotted line.
12 Will complete a line of horizontal dots of 3 in. when given a verbal prompt.
13 Will complete a line of horizontal dots of 4 in. when teacher holds child's hand and does it with him/her.
14 Will complete a line of horizontal dots of 4 in. when given a physical prompt.
15 Will complete a line of horizontal dots of 4 in. when given a verbal prompt.
16 Will copy a horizontal line of 4 in. given a physical prompt.
17 Will copy a horizontal line of 4 in. given a verbal prompt.

Drawing lines between lines

Techniques
Prompting
Fading

Objectives

1 Will draw a line of 4 in. horizontally in between two lines 3 in. apart with physical prompt.

2   Will draw a line of 4 in. horizontally in between two lines 3 in. apart with verbal prompt.
3   Will draw a line of 4 in. horizontally in between two lines 2½ in. apart with physical prompt.
4   Will draw a line of 4 in. horizontally in between two lines 2½ in. apart with verbal prompt.
5   Will draw a line of 4 in. horizontally in between two lines 2 in. apart with physical prompt.
6   Will draw a line of 4 in. horizontally in between two lines 2 in. apart with verbal prompt.
7   Will draw a line of 4 in. in between two lines 1½ in. apart given a physical prompt.
8   Will draw a line of 4 in. in between two lines 1½ in. apart given a verbal prompt.
9   Will draw a line of 4 in. in between two lines 1 in. apart given a physical prompt.
10 Will draw a line of 4 in. in between two lines 1 in. apart given a verbal prompt.

Copying large shapes: square

Techniques
Chaining
Fading

Objectives
1   Will complete one side of 4 in. square with dots.
2   Will complete two sides of 4 in. square with dots.
3   Will complete three sides of 4 in. square with dots.
4   Will complete four sides of 4 in. square with dots.
5   Will complete one side of 4 in. square with no dots.
6   Will complete two sides of 4 in. square with no dots.
7   Will complete three sides of 4 in. square with no dots.
8   Will copy a 4 in. square with four dots marking each point.

Copying small shapes: square

Objectives
1   Will complete one side of a 2 in. square with dots.
2   Will complete two sides of a 2 in. square with dots.
3   Will complete three sides of a 2 in. square with dots.
4   Will complete four sides of a 2 in. square with dots.
5   Will complete one side of a 2 in. square with no dots.
6   Will complete two sides of a 2 in. square with no dots.
7   Will complete three sides of a 2 in. square with no dots.
8   Will copy a 2 in. square with a dot marking each point.

(As above for other shapes.)

Copying letters: 'E'

Techniques
Chaining
Fading

Objectives
1 Will complete ⊢ one arm of letter 'E' with dots.
2 Will complete ⊢ two arms of letter 'E' with dots.
3 Will complete ⊢ three arms of letter 'E' with dots.
4 Will complete   entire letter 'E' with dots.
5 Will copy letter 'E'.

(As above if using lower case letters or any other letters.)

Copying name: DARREN

Techniques
Chaining
Fading

Objectives
1 Will complete first name in upper case letters with dots.
2 Will complete first name in upper case letters with only last letter missing: D A R R E _ from model.
3 Will complete first name in upper case letters with last two letters missing: D A R R _ _ from model.
4 Will complete first name in upper case letters with last three letters missing: D A R _ _ _ from model.
5 Will complete first name in upper case letters with last four letters missing: D A _ _ _ _ from model.
6 Will complete first name in upper case letters with last five letters missing: D _ _ _ _ _ from model.
7 Will copy first name from model.

(As above for lower case letters and last name.)

You will need to prepare a booklet for each stage of the programmes 1 to 7 with enough examples of each step so that you can record and evaluate. I would give him or her ten such examples per day.

Example: Forming letters

The following programme was constructed for a young ten-year-old boy, P.J., in a class for the E.S.N. (M) pupil. He was functioning at a much lower level and needed a great deal of external reinforcement together with task analysis. He could hold a pencil and was able to make horizontal, vertical and circular marks. He was also able to discriminate. He had difficulty copying. Our objectives for one letter, 'e', were as follows:

Techniques
Fading
Backward chaining

Objectives
1   P.J. will complete the letter 'e' when presented with ⊙ , following a demonstration.
2   P.J. will complete the letter 'e' when presented with ⊙ , when told to finish the 'e'.
3   P.J. will complete the letter 'e' when presented with ⊙ , following a demonstration.
4   P.J. will do above when asked to "finish the 'e'".
5   P.J. will complete the letter 'e' when presented with ⊙ , following a demonstration.
6   P.J. will do above when told to "finish the 'e'".
7   P.J. will complete the letter 'e' when presented with ⊙ , when told "go over the dots and make an 'e'".
8   P.J. will form the letter 'e' when presented with ⊙ , and asked to form the letter.
9   P.J. will form the letter 'e' when given a red dot as a visual cue to start from.
10 P.J. will copy an 'e' from a model.

His teacher made up a booklet with several pages for each step of the programme. P.J. was given one minute every day to complete as many of the semi-formed letters as he could. A record was kept of his successes and errors.

The results are shown in Fig. 7. P.J. not only completed more letters as the days went by, but his success rate also increased to the maximum possible.

This is a variation of a technique also known as 'Precision Teaching', and an excellent classroom manual has been produced by Williams *et al* (1980) for teachers.

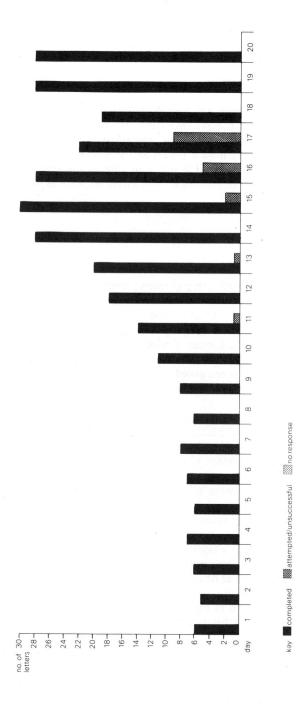

Fig. 7 Forming the letter 'e': pupil P.J.

key ■ completed   ▨ attempted/unsuccessful   ▧ no response

7 Communication

The variety of handicap in an E.S.N. (S) school means that several different systems of communication need to be taught, and at different levels. These include gestures, sign systems, speech, and combinations of each. The following are useful texts in this area: Jeffree & McConkey (1976); Kiernan *et al* (1978); and Shiack (1974).

A RECEPTIVE LANGUAGE/UNDERSTANDING

Our objectives in this area are sequenced in such a way that we would expect a child to progress through the objectives in the order in which they are set out.

Objectives
1 Responds to single-component command with appropriate motor action, e.g. 'Come here.'
2 Responds to two-component command with appropriate motor action, e.g. 'Come here, and look at me.'
3 Responds to three-component command with appropriate motor action, e.g. 'Come here, look at me, and sit down.'
4 Will point to named object in an array of two objects.
5 Will point to named object in an array of three objects, etc.
6 Will fetch named objects increasing in number.
7 Will point to one named body part.
8 Will point to two named body parts.
9 Will point to three named body parts, etc.
10 Will point to named colours.
11 Will point to size concepts 'big', 'little'.
12 Will point to named objects in a picture.
13 Will point to sets of objects involving number, e.g. 'Show me the group of five flowers.'
14 Will match objects when asked, 'Show me the two that are the same.'
15 Will match pictures when asked, 'Show me the two that are the same.'
16 Will pick out/point to an object which is different from others in an array, e.g. varying shape, size, colour, texture.
17 Will repeat theme of a three/four-sentence utterance.
18 Will tell the main events of a short story in any order.
19 Will tell main events of a short story in the correct order.

The previous analysis is only one example of how 'understanding' can be taught by objectives. However, the step size between each objective is rather large for an E.S.N. (S) child, and below, some of the objectives are graded more finely.

Objectives 4 and 5

Will point to a named object in an array of two objects.
Will point to a named object in an array of three objects.

The following programme was constructed for J.D., a girl of ten years with no speech and a very short attention span. She was known to like apples and a picture of an apple was chosen as the target object. She could already recognize the real object and it was felt that a symbolic representation of it would be an appropriate next step to aim for in J.D.'s receptive vocabulary.

Technique
Errorless discrimination learning

Objectives
1   Will give teacher a picture of an apple placed on a table with no other pictures present, on request.
2   Will give teacher the picture of an apple when presented with one other picture (not representing food), in rotated positions.
3   Will give teacher the picture of an apple when presented with two other dissimilar pictures.
4   Will give teacher the picture of an apple when presented with three other dissimilar pictures.

The results of the programme after nine weeks are presented in Fig. 8. It can be seen that J.D. found it difficult to cope with the increased level of difficulty with the progression of the programme. However, her rate of 'attempts' rose steeply in the eighth and ninth week indicating an approximation to the 75 per cent criterion.

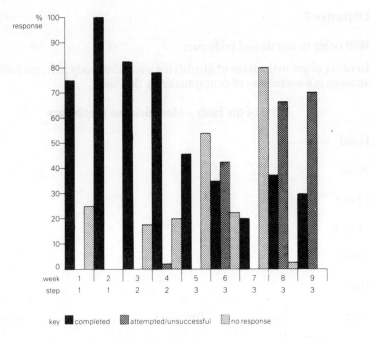

Fig. 8 Receptive vocabulary (pointing to apple): pupil J.D.

key ■ completed ▨ attempted/unsuccessful ▧ no response

Objective 7

Will point to one named body part.

In order to get to the stage of identifying a specified body part, the following analysis is a useful way of conceptualizing this task:

Parts of the body – identification vocabulary

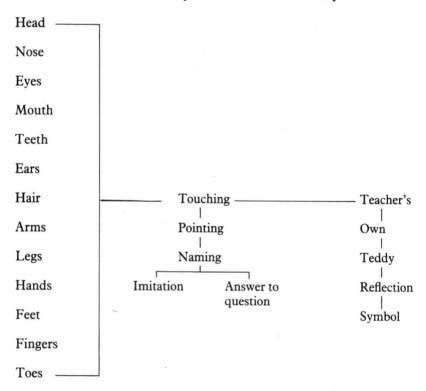

Taking 'head' as the first body part, the following objectives can be written for a child who will need maximum guidance and practice. Note that this programme begins with receptive vocabulary but moves on to expressive language. Where it is suspected that a pupil will not be able to use speech, a sign can be substituted where appropriate. The 'naming' of the body part could be taught at a much later date if it is assumed that the pupil will be able to verbalize but is not at present ready to.

A   TOUCHING HEAD: TEACHER'S
1   Will touch teacher's head when teacher holds his/her hand and guides him/her.

2   Will touch teacher's head in response to a command, when given a slight physical prompt.
3   Will touch teacher's head when asked to.

B   POINTING TO HEAD: TEACHER'S
1   Will point to teacher's head when teacher holds his/her hand and guides him/her using preferred hand.
2   Will point to teacher's head in response to a command, when teacher gives a slight physical prompt.
3   Will point to teacher's head when given a command.

C   TOUCHING OWN HEAD
1   Will touch own head when teacher holds his/her hand and guides him/her.
2   Will touch own head in response to a command, when teacher gives a slight physical prompt.
3   Will touch own head when asked to.

D   POINTING TO OWN HEAD
1   Will point to own head when teacher holds his/her hand and guides him/her using preferred hand.
2   Will point to own head in response to a command, given a slight physical prompt.
3   Will point to own head when given a command.

E   TOUCHING TEDDY'S HEAD
1   Will touch teddy's head when teacher holds his/her hand and guides him/her.
2   Will touch teddy's head when teacher gives a slight physical prompt in response to a command.
3   Will touch teddy's head when asked to do so.

F   POINTING TO TEDDY'S HEAD
1   Will point to teddy's head when teacher holds his/her hand and guides him/her, with preferred hand.
2   Will point to teddy's head when teacher gives a slight physical prompt, in response to a command.
3   Will point to teddy's head when asked to do so.

(As above for reflection and picture.)

G   NAMING 'HEAD'
1   Will say 'head' in imitation when teacher holds his/her hand and guides it to her head.
2   Will say 'head' in imitation when teacher holds his/her hand and guides it to his/her own head.

3 Will say 'head' in imitation when teacher holds his/her hand and guides it to teddy's head.
4 Will say 'head' in imitation when teacher holds his/her hand and guides it to a reflection in the mirror.
5 Will say 'head' in imitation when teacher holds his/her hand and guides it to a picture of a head.
6 Will say 'head' when teacher points to her own head and asks 'What is this?'
7 Will say 'head' when teacher points to child's head and asks 'What is this?'
8 Will say 'head' when teacher points to teddy's head and asks 'What is this?'
9 Will say 'head' when teacher points to a reflection of a head and asks 'What is this?'
10 Will say 'head' when teacher points to a picture of a head and asks 'What is this?'
11 As above in random order.

The above analysis can be repeated exactly for the remaining parts of the body. It is possible to omit the pointing programme if this is felt to be superfluous, although one must distinguish between Touching and Pointing especially as you are teaching this pupil skills within the Hand–eye Co-ordination area.

When recording, state exactly what programme you are on, plus what step on that programme, so that proper evaluation can be made.

Objective 16

Will pick out/point to an object which is different from others in an array.

A VARYING SHAPE – USING ERRORLESS DISCRIMINATION LEARNING
Techniques
Errorless discrimination learning
Prompting

Equipment
Beakers
Spoons
Dolls
Cars

Objectives
1 Will touch *car* when adult places child's hand on car saying, 'This one is different,' in an array of spoons.
2 As above with slight physical prompt.

3   As above with verbal prompt.
4   Will touch *doll* in an array of beakers when adult places child's hand on doll saying, 'This one is different.'
5   Will do above with slight physical prompt.
6   Will do above with verbal prompt.
7   Will touch *beaker* in an array of dolls when adult places child's hand on beaker saying, 'This one is different.'
8   As above with slight physical prompt.
9   As above with verbal prompt.
10 Will touch *spoon* in array of cars when adult places child's hand on spoon and says, 'This one is different.'
11 Will do above with slight physical prompt.
12 Will do above with verbal prompt.
13 Will point to each of objects in turn when asked, 'Show me which one is different.'

B   VARYING SIZE – USING ERRORLESS DISCRIMINATION LEARNING AND PROMPTING

Equipment
Large blocks and small blocks
Large sticks and small sticks
Large beads and small beads
Large biscuits and small biscuits
Large bar of chocolate and one piece of chocolate

Objectives
1   Will touch large *block* when in array of small blocks when adult places child's hand on large block saying, 'This one is different.'
2   As above with slight physical prompt.
3   As above with verbal prompt.
4   Will touch large *stick* when in array of small sticks, when adult places child's hand on large stick saying, 'This one is different.'
6   As above with verbal prompt.
7   Will touch large *bead* when in array of small beads, when adult places child's hand on large bead saying, 'This one is different.'
8   As above with slight physical prompt.
9   As above with verbal prompt.

(As above for remaining items.)

Note that steps 1–3 can be repeated for 'small block'; steps 4–6 for 'small stick', etc.

A similar technique can be used for objective 11 – 'Will point to size concepts of "big" and "little".'

Objective 14

Will match objects when asked, 'Show me the two that are the same.'

Techniques
Errorless discrimination learning
Prompting

Equipment
Biscuits
Pieces of cloth
Sponges
Toy cars

1   Will pick out and place together two *sponges* adjacent to each other in an array of three objects, when adult takes child's hands and places them on the sponges saying, 'These two are the same.'
2   As above with slight physical prompt.
3   As above with verbal prompt.
4   Will pick out and place together two sponges separated by one object when adult places child's hand on sponges saying, 'These two are the same.'
5   As above with slight physical prompt.
6   As above with verbal prompt.
7   Will pick out and place together two sponges when separated by two objects, when adult places child's hands on sponges saying, 'These two are the same.'
8   As above with slight physical prompt.
9   As above with verbal prompt.
    (etc.)

The same objectives can be written for the remaining items of biscuits, cars, etc.

The following programme was constructed for D.W., an eleven-year-old girl of very limited ability. She was able to use two-word utterances. She was also able to sit down and perform hand–eye tasks, for example, inset boards, puzzles, etc. It was decided to teach her to match objects using other dissimilar objects in the first stage, and similar objects in the second stage but of varying size and shape.

Task
To match objects when asked, 'Show me two things that are the same.'

Techniques
Prompting
Fading
Errorless discrimination learning

Objects
Bottle
Toothbrush
2 Beakers (target)

Stage 1
(Using dissimilar objects)
1 Will point to one item on request.
2 Will point to one item and name it on request.
3 Will point to two identical items (beakers) with modelling and physical guidance.
4 Will point to two identical items (beakers) with a physical prompt.
5 Will point to two identical items (beakers) when given a verbal command.
6 Will pick out and place together two identical items (beakers) when separated by one dissimilar object (bottle) when teacher places D.W.'s hands on the beakers and says, 'These are the same.'
7 As above with physical prompt.
8 As above with a verbal prompt.
9 Will pick out and place together two identical items (beakers) when separated by two dissimilar objects (bottle, toothbrush) when teacher places D.W.'s hands on the beakers saying, 'These are the same.'
10 As above with a physical prompt.
11 As above with a verbal prompt.
12 Will pick out and place together *two* identical items (beakers) when in the following array: beaker; bottle; beaker; toothbrush; with a physical prompt.
13 As above with verbal prompt.

Fig. 9 presents the results of this programme which took ten weeks to complete to the 75 per cent criterion level of success per step. D.W. seemed to take five weeks to achieve a 75 per cent level of success on step 4, but then was able to skip a few steps without loss of performance.

Teacher's comments
Although it appeared that D.W. would find this task too difficult, it was pleasant to find her moving on so quickly after the plateau reached on step 4. It was helpful having such a finely graded programme in the initial stages as it was seen to be necssary in this case. It was easier towards the final stages to skip some steps, particularly those involving physical prompting as they were not then necessary. It was encouraging to see D.W.'s progress on this task and a similar format was then adopted for other objects.

D.W.'s teacher went on to teach D.W. matching similar objects, e.g. toothbrush and hairbrush; different types of bottles, etc. Later a colour matching programme was constructed for D.W.

Fig. 10 presents the results of the progress on the same programme made

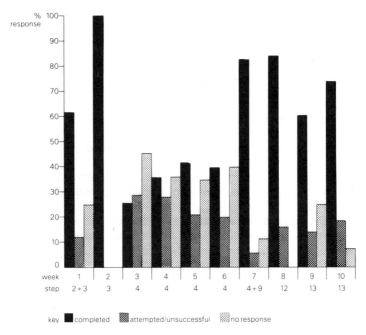

Fig. 9 Matching two identical yellow beakers: pupil D.W.

by M.L., a girl of ten years who was able to make one or two word utterances and had good manipulative skills. It was felt that 'concept' programmes of 'same' and 'different' would be useful to teach her so that she could move on to higher order tasks. M.L. took sixteen weeks to complete the programme at the 75 per cent criterion of success per step. Her progress was much steadier than that of D.W., although it took her three weeks to progress through each of steps 2 and 3. The programme was basic and detailed enough to be carried out by a nursery nurse.

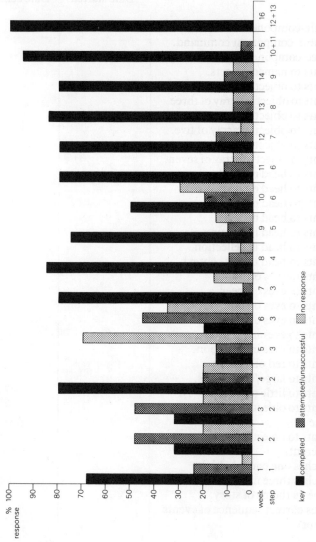

Fig. 10 Matching two identical yellow beakers: pupil M.L.

Sample record sheet

UNDERSTANDING OF LANGUAGE

		Date started	Date achieved
1	Single-component command.		
2	Double-component command.		
3	Three-component command.		
4	Points to named objects.		
5	Points to object in array of two.		
6	Points to object in array of three.		
7	Points to object in array of four.		
8	Points to object in array of five.		
9	Points to object in array of six.		
10	Points to object in array of seven.		
11	Points to head on adult.		
12	Points to head on peer.		
13	Points to head on doll.		
14	Points to head on self.		
15	Points to head in picture.		
16	Points to head in reflection.		
17	Points to head in any context.		
18	Points to eyes on adult.		
19	Points to eyes on peer.		
20	Points to eyes on doll.		
21	Points to eyes on self.		
22	Points to eyes in picture.		
23	Points to eyes in reflection.		
24	Points to red objects.		
25	Points to large/big objects.		
26	Points to little objects.		
27	Points to objects that are the same.		
28	Points to objects that are different.		
29	Fetches one named object.		
30	Fetches three named objects.		
31	Repeats theme of story.		
32	Gives correct sequence of events in story.		

B EXPRESSIVE LANGUAGE

In this section, the objectives are once again sequenced in an order such that we assume that learning one will help in reaching future targets. It is usual to set out objectives in a developmental order, but teaching them may not be that simple with certain children. They may not develop speech in quite the same way as a normal child. For example, many programmes include the teaching of every consonant and vowel sound in isolation. However, this may not have a direct carry over into the production of words for some children. Care needs to be taken, when writing programmes, to allow for flexibility.

Techniques
Modelling
Prompting
Shaping
Immediate reinforcement

Objectives
A   WORDS AND PHRASES
1   Will imitate vowel sounds, e.g. 'eee,' 'aaa,' 'ooo'. (Reinforce.)
2   Will imitate consonants. (Reinforce.)
3   Will imitate one-syllable words, e.g. 'car'. (Reinforce.)
4   Will imitate two-syllable words, e.g. 'table'. (Reinforce.)
5   Will imitate three-syllable words, e.g. 'telephone'. (Reinforce.)
6   Will imitate one-, two- and three-syllable noun words consecutively. (Reinforce.)
7   Will imitate two-word phrase, using noun and verb, e.g. 'car go'. (Reinforce.)
8   Will imitate three-word phrase, using noun and verb and preposition, e.g. 'car go in'. (Reinforce.)
9   Will imitate four-word phrase using noun and verb and preposition and adverb, e.g. 'car go in quick'. (Reinforce.)
10 Will repeat five-word phrase using noun and verb and preposition and adverb and adjective, e.g. 'red car go in quick'. (Reinforce.)
11 Will use pronouns.

The above sequence of objectives reflects the way in which a very young child would begin to speak. There is some controversy about whether or not it is advisable to teach a child to use the definite article, 'the', and whether or not they should be taught to produce phrases/sentences which are grammatically correct, but may not actually be used in everyday speech. For example, if asked, 'What is this?', a child or adult would reply 'a ......'. To teach a child, especially one with severe learning difficulties, to say, 'This is a ......' is probably over-ambitious and in many cases redundant. However, it depends very much on the teacher's personal preference and standards. For useful assessment schedules on imitation see Kiernan & Jones (1977).

B   SENTENCES
1   Will imitate identity statements, e.g. 'This is a book.' (Reinforce.)
2   Will complete identity statements, e.g. 'This is . . . .' (Reinforce.)
3   Will answer question using an identity statement, e.g. 'This is a book' in response to 'What is this?'
4   Uses identity statement including an adjective, e.g. 'This is a heavy book' in imitation. (Reinforce.)
5   As above, completing the sentence 'This is . . . .' (Reinforce.)
6   Will say 'This book feels heavy' in response to question 'What does the book feel like?' (Reinforce.)
7   Will imitate a sentence using an action statement, e.g. 'The girl is eating.' (Reinforce.)
8   Will complete sentence using action statement, e.g. 'The girl . . . .' (Reinforce.)
9   Will say, 'The girl is eating', or 'She is eating' in response to question 'What is the girl doing?' (Reinforce.)
10 Will answer question using personal pronouns, e.g. will say, 'I am colouring' in response to question 'What are you doing?' (Reinforce.)
11 Will use other pronouns when they are used in questions, e.g. will say 'He is angry' in response to question 'What is he feeling?' (Reinforce.)

C   LANGUAGE OF CATEGORIES — EMOTION
1   Will imitate sentences expressing emotion when shown in a picture, e.g. 'The little boy is happy.' (Reinforce.)
2   Will answer question about picture reflecting emotion, in response to 'How is the boy feeling?' by saying 'He is feeling happy.' (Reinforce.)
3   Will give reason for emotion in picture in imitation, e.g. 'The little boy is happy because he has a new bike.' (Reinforce.)
4   Will say above sentence in response to question 'Why is the boy happy?' (Reinforce.)

(As above for other emotions being taught.)

Similar series of objectives can be written for the language of: Food; Clothes; Toys; Transport; Scenery; Leisure; Furniture; Rooms at home; etc.

Remember to include steps of: (a) imitation, (b) completion, (c) answering questions.

The following programme was constructed for a boy, D.D. aged six years. He was retarded in all areas of development, with a language age of eighteen months. He was noticed to have begun to imitate sounds, and was making some spontaneous speech sounds, for example, imitating the sound of a car. He was adept at making his needs known using non-verbal signals. One of D.D.'s problems was that of eye contact with an adult, which gave rise to doubts about his listening and attention skills. A programme to get him to attend, listen and imitate names of familiar objects was therefore drawn up.

Expressive language programme for D.D.

Aim: To build up vocabulary

Task
Naming objects

Objects
Stage 1 = toys
Stage 2 = utility objects
Stage 3 = food

Basal level
D.D. can do the following early stages: Will give six specified toys to adult when asked, 'Give me the cat/car/fish/doll/horse/ball.' All objects were chosen because D.D. was familiar with them.

Stage 1

(a) Imitation using modelling

Criterion: 75 per cent per step per week.

1   Will say 'cat' when teacher points to cat and says, 'This is a cat' with *no* other objects present.
2   Will say 'cat' when teacher points to cat and says, 'This is a cat' with a car present.
3   Will say 'car' when teacher points to the car and says 'This is a car' with a cat present.
4   Will say 'cat' and 'car' in succession when teacher points to each in turn saying, 'This is a cat' and 'This is a car.'
5   Will say 'fish' when teacher points to the fish and says, 'This is a fish' with *no* other objects present.
6   Will say 'fish' when teacher points to the fish and says, 'This is a fish' with a cat and car present.
7   Will say 'cat' when teacher points to the cat and says, 'This is a cat' with the car and fish present.
8   Will say 'car' when teacher points to car and says, 'This is a car' with the cat and fish present.
9   Will say 'doll' when teacher points to doll and says, 'This is a doll' when *no* other objects are present.
10 Will say 'doll' when teacher points to doll and says, 'This is a doll' with the cat, car and fish present.
11 Will say 'cat' when teacher points to the cat and says, 'This is a cat' with the car, fish and doll present.
12 Will say 'car' when teacher points to the car and says, 'This is a car' with the cat, fish and doll present.

13 Will say 'fish' when the teacher points to the fish and says, 'This is a fish' with the cat, car and doll present.
14 Will say 'horse' when teacher points to the horse and says, 'This is a horse' with *no* other objects present.
15 Will say 'horse' when teacher points to the horse and says, 'This is a horse' with the cat, car, fish and doll present.
16 Will say 'cat' when teacher points to the cat and says, 'This is a cat' with the car, fish, doll and horse present.
17 Will say 'car' when teacher points to the car and says, 'This is a car' with the cat, fish, doll and horse present.
18 Will say 'fish' when teacher points to the fish and says, 'This is a fish' with the cat, car, doll and horse present.
19 Will say 'doll' when teacher points to the doll and says, 'This is a doll' with the cat, car, fish and horse present.
20 Will say 'ball' when teacher points to the ball and says, 'This is a ball' with *no* other objects present.
21 Will say 'ball' when teacher points to the ball and says, 'This is a ball' with the cat, car, fish, doll and horse present.
22 Will say each object in imitation when all are present, in succession.
23 Will say each object in imitation when all are present, in different positions.

(b) Answering a question

Criterion: 4–5 a day

1   Will say 'cat' in response to the question 'What is this?' when shown the cat with *no* other objects present.
2   Will say 'car' in response to the question 'What is this?' when shown the car with *no* other objects present.
3   Will say 'fish' in response to the question 'What is this?' when shown the fish, with *no* other objects present.
4   Will say 'doll' in response to the question 'What is this?' when shown the doll with *no* other objects present.
5   Will say 'horse' in response to the question 'What is this?' when shown the horse with *no* other objects present.
6   Will say 'ball' in response to the question 'What is this?' when shown the ball with *no* other objects present.
7   Will say 'cat' in response to the question 'What is this?' when shown the cat with the car present.
8   Will say 'car' when teacher points to car and says, 'What is this?' with the cat present.
9   Will say 'fish' in response to the question 'What is this?' with the cat and the car present.
10 Will say 'cat' in response to the question 'What is this?' with the car and the fish present.
11 Will say 'car' in response to the question 'What is this?' with the cat and

fish present.

12 Will say 'doll' in response to the question 'What is this?' with the cat, car and fish present.

13 Will say 'cat' in response to the question 'What is this?' with the car, fish and doll present.

14 Will say 'car' in response to the question 'What is this?' with the cat, fish and doll present.

15 Will say 'fish' in response to the question 'What is this?' with the cat, car and doll present.

16 Will say 'horse' in response to the question 'What is this?' with the cat, car, fish and doll present.

17 Will say 'cat' in response to the question 'What is this?' with the car, doll, fish and horse present.

18 Will say 'car' in response to the question 'What is this?' with the cat, doll, fish and horse present.

19 Will say 'doll' in response to the question 'What is this?' with the cat, car, fish and horse present.

20 Will say 'fish' in response to the question 'What is this?' with the cat, car, doll and horse present.

21 Will say 'ball' in response to the question 'What is this?' with the cat, car, doll, fish and horse present.

22 Will say 'cat' in response to the question 'What is this?' with the car, doll, fish, horse and ball present.

23 Will say 'car' in response to the question 'What is this?' with the cat, fish, doll, horse and ball present.

24 Will say 'fish' in response to the question 'What is this?' with the cat, car, doll, horse and ball present.

25 Will say 'doll' in response to the question 'What is this?' with the cat, car, fish, horse and ball present.

26 Will say 'horse' in response to the question 'What is this?' with the cat, car, fish, doll and ball present.

27 Will say the name of each object in turn when asked 'What is this?' when objects are placed in different positions.

The results of the programme after eleven weeks are presented in Fig. 11. It can be seen that by about the fifth week, D.D. had grasped the nature of the task and was performing at the 80 per cent level of success which he maintained and increased for the next few weeks.

Teacher's comments
D.D.'s teacher was pleased at the response she got from D.D. However, she noted that he would use the words out of context during the time he was not on the programme. His level of spontaneous speech was heard to increase. It was very difficult to get D.D. to respond during the actual operation of the programme. His teacher made a note of when he did use the words in context spontaneously.

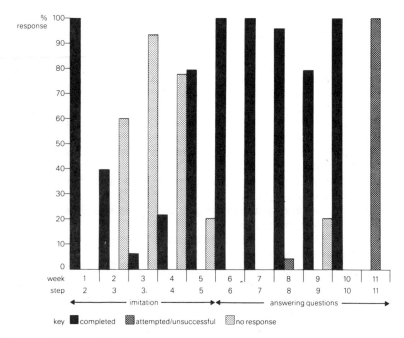

Fig. 11 Expressive language programme – naming objects by imitating and answering questions: pupil D.D.

D COMBINATION SENTENCES
1 Will imitate a sentence (using a picture) with food and furniture nouns, e.g. 'I ate my cornflakes at the table.'
2 Will make up sentence combining food and furniture nouns, when given pictures reflecting those nouns.
3 Will imitate a sentence using transport and leisure concepts, e.g. 'I went in a bus to the park and played.'
4 Will make up a sentence using the above concepts, given pictures reflecting them.

(As above for other combinations.)

E   FUNCTIONAL SPEECH

1   Will name food/drink when child wants it, e.g. squash, chocolate, cake. (Reinforce.)
2   Will say 'more . . . . . .' when eating food/drink item. (Reinforce.)
3   Will say 'toilet' when wishing to use toilet. (Reinforce.)
4   Will name toy child wants to play with, e.g. 'bike'. (Reinforce.)
5   Will ask adult to 'look . . . . . .' when wanting attention or approval or to share something. (Reinforce.)
6   Will say 'off' when wishing for clothing to be removed. (Reinforce.)
7   Will say 'TV.' (Reinforce.)
8   Will use nouns appropriately, e.g. 'car' for all cars but not for dolls, etc. (Reinforce.)

For examples of programmes see Jeffree and McConkey (1976) and Shiack (1974).

The actual training of 'spontaneous' functional speech depends very much on the response of the adult after the child has vocalized. For instance, if the child says, 'tea' he must get the tea immediately so that he associates the word and drink, and will be more likely to say it again. He should not be given the tea if he has made no attempt to say the word. Similarly, if the wrong word has been used, you must correct him, and get him to imitate the correct word. Avoid giving the child attention for incorrect speech or no speech during training phases. (Of course, the reward should only be withheld during the period of training, and not generally.)

Sample record sheet

EXPRESSIVE LANGUAGE

		Date started	Date achieved
1	Imitates long vowel sounds.		
2	'b' as in boy		
	'm' as in man		
	'd' as in dog		
	'n' as in no		
	'p' as in pipe		
	's' as in see		
	'f' as in fat		
	'g' as in go		
	'k' as in cat		
	'h' as in hat		
	't' as in toy		
	'w' as in way		
	'j' as in jug		
	'l' as in look		
	'q' as in quick		
	'r' as in road		
	'v' as in vest		
3	Imitates one-syllable word.		
4	Imitates two-syllable word.		
5	Imitates three-syllable word.		
6	Imitates one-, two- and three-syllable word.		
7	Imitates two-word phrase.		
8	Imitates three-word phrase.		
9	Imitates four-word phrase.		
10	Imitates five-word phrase.		
11	Uses personal pronoun.		
12	Imitates identity statement.		
13	Completes identity statement.		
14	Answers question giving identity statement.		
15	Imitates action statement.		
16	Completes action statement.		
17	Answers question giving action statement.		
18	Uses other pronoun.		

8 Non-verbal communication

Non-verbal communication is a very important aspect of the whole communication process. While most children and adults use the skills of non-verbal communication in an automatic fashion, handicapped individuals may need training in this area. With severe learning difficulties, handicapped children may not be able to use the information in the environment provided by those with whom they are interacting, and therefore need to be guided so as to become more aware of such signals. They may then be able to respond accordingly, and to use them appropriately themselves.

The component skills of non-verbal communication include eye contact, body posture, body proximity, facial expressions, and gestures.

Eye contact

Objectives (1st order analysis)
1 Will look at listener before speaking.
2 Will look at listener just before completing utterance.
3 Will look at listener on and off while speaking.
4 Will look at speaker before being spoken to.
5 Will look at speaker before it is his/her turn to speak.
6 Will look at speaker on and off while being addressed.

Objectives (3rd order analysis)

Techniques
Shaping
Prompting
Immediate reinforcement

1 Will look at speaker when speaker (teacher) holds child's head up and smiles at child, giving verbal reinforcement.
2 As above, maintaining gaze for three seconds, getting a smile and verbal reinforcement.
3 Will respond to physical contact or speech by looking at adult (teacher), reinforced by smiles and conversation.

In general, eye contact between individuals is reinforcing in itself. Simply returning the child's gaze, nodding, smiling or addressing him/her can be all the reward that is needed. The pleasure that the child gets from the contact with the adult should encourage him/her to engage in further eye contact. Where a child initiates contact without eye contact (head bowed or face turned away) an adult should give no response. This will 'shape' the child's behaviour, so that he/she will learn that he/she will only gain contact with another person if they engage in appropriate eye contact.

Body posture

Objectives (1st order analysis)
1   Will face speaker while being addressed.
2   Will face a listener while speaking.
3   Will incline body towards the listener.
4   Will incline body towards the speaker.
5   Will unfold arms in an open fashion towards the speaker.
6   As step 5 to listener.
7   Will open mouth sufficiently when speaking.
8   Will uncover mouth by removing hands from mouth when speaking.
9   Will keep head in the upright position.

Training in the area of body posture involves making pupils aware of their own behaviour when they are communicating with others. It can be done by making a video tape of real or role played situations. The ideal situation would involve a video tape where the tape could be stopped at the relevant points to emphasize certain postures. However, it can be done by simply conducting role play sessions meaningful to the children. These sessions could be of particular use to older pupils as they prepare to meet adults who may not be aware of their handicap. It will of course be vital for those pupils who will be engaging in interviews with careers officers, managers of industrial units, colleges of further education and the staff within, managers of sheltered workshops or the full range of employers in the employment market.

Pupils should be encouraged to note the consequences of their body posture and eye contact. Did a certain posture make the interviewer feel as if the pupil were being aggressive, or unconcerned? Did the pupil manage to convey what it was that he/she intended? How do they know? Could they have adopted any other postures that would have changed the nature of the interaction? Reversed role play in this instance is a very helpful device for pupils to appreciate how the interviewer felt, and vice versa. For those pupils who are shy or withdrawn the feedback they receive from role play exercises can be very valuable in helping them gain confidence, and to try and alter those aspects of their behaviour that are causing them difficulty in social situations.

For those pupils who tend to get flustered when asked about themselves, being given feedback about how their behaviour was perceived in any particular situation can help them to correct their posture, etc. Along with body posture, eye contact and proximity, it is important to notice how a pupil breathes when communicating, as this alone can give others the impression of nervousness, excitability, boredom or unconcern. Fast shallow breathing can indicate nervousness and excitability, while long deep sighs can indicate boredom or unconcern. Simple breathing exercises can be used to control these behaviours if they give an unfavourable impression.

Body proximity

In general individuals should not sit or stand too close to strangers or those they do not know intimately. With those whom they know well, or are about to engage in conversation/interaction with, they should stand within hearing distance. Many pupils who have learning difficulties can experience difficulties distinguishing between those with whom they should maintain a reasonable distance, and those with whom it is acceptable to be close to, hold hands, embrace, etc. The best technique for training these skills is that of shaping, where the pupil gets immediate reinforcement for behaving in an acceptable manner, and ignored if behaving in an unacceptable way. The reinforcement is eye contact, interesting facial expression, and body inclined towards the child. This is a vital skill for pupils who already engage in community life, or who are about to. Body proximity is usually the one aspect of communication which can so easily be misinterpreted by those not aware of an individual's handicap.

Facial expressions

These refer to smiles, frowns, looks of surprise, boredom, annoyance, etc. It must be stressed, however, that a facial expression is only one cue to the way a person feels at that moment in time. All the other aspects of non-verbal communication are also taken into account by the observer. For the express purposes of this text, it is being broken down into its component parts. Facial expressions are very important as observers tend to look at the face first, and then the rest of the body, to make sure that the message being received is consistent or congruent. Some pupils may give little expression, and make communication difficult, while others may give messages with their faces that they never intended to do. For example it is very easy to confuse the signs for embarrassment and shyness or even a smirky type of expression.

The best way to make pupils aware of the expressions they use in social encounters is firstly by making sure that they themselves can decipher what certain facial expressions signify. Miming exercises are helpful here, for example, charades. Matching emotions to facial expressions on a bingo game type format is also valuable. Next, pupils should be encouraged to role play each other, to provide the necessary feedback. They should first be asked to role play in a situation and then watch some other pupil playing them. This way they can discover if the messages they intended to give were in fact received. They can then practise giving the proper signals for the situation in hand.

Gestures

For those who for some reason are unable to produce speech, the use of gesture is useful, especially if they are going to be taught a signing system later on.

Techniques
Modelling
Shaping
Immediate reinforcement

Objectives
(Reinforce after every trial.)
1 Will shake head for 'no'.
2 Will nod head for 'yes'.
3 Will point to items wanted.
4 Will pull adult to wanted item.
5 Will hold self to indicate toilet need.
6 Will mime drinking action to indicate need for drink.
7 Will push away plate when finished eating.
8 Will turn head away from unpleasant stimulus.
9 Waves goodbye.
10 Claps to show pleasure.
11 Smiles to show pleasure.

Many of the above may have to be modelled, and repeated with a variety of items in the case of objectives 3 and 4. Immediate reinforcement is vital in training these skills.

Playing charades and other miming games can be an interesting way of teaching pupils to use gestures. Here peers become the agents who model a particular behaviour that other pupils can be encouraged to imitate. With the more severely handicapped, adults will have to give a great deal of physical prompting for children to realize that imitation is what is required of them and that it will get them the required object to satisfy their immediate need. Training in eye contact and attention skills will be a necessary precursor to the training of gesture skills.

9　Cognitive skills

A　COLOUR

There are probably two elements in teaching the concept of colour. Provided the pupil is not colour blind, the first stage should be for the child to recognize colours, and then the second stage would be to name them.

Techniques
Errorless discrimination learning
Overlearning

Equipment
6 blocks of equal size, red, yellow, blue, green, black, white

Objectives
A　TO POINT TO 'RED' USING ONE TYPE OF OBJECT
1　Will point to a *red* block when asked to point to the red block with no other object present.
2　Will point to a *red* block with a blue block present on the right of the red, when asked.
3　Will point to a *red* block with a blue block present on the left of the red, when asked.
4　Will point to a *red* block with a blue block and yellow block on either side, when asked.
5　Will point to a *red* block with the blue and yellow blocks to the right of the red, when asked.
6　Will point to a *red* block with the red block on the right of the other two, when asked.
7　Will point to the *red* block when presented with blue, yellow and green blocks in addition, when asked.
8　Will point to the *red* block when presented with the blue, yellow and green ones in different positions, when asked.
9　Will point to the *red* block when presented with blue, yellow, green and white blocks in different positions, when asked.
10　Will point to the *red* block when presented with blue, yellow, green, white and black ones in different positions, when asked.

(As above for remaining colours.)

B　TO POINT TO 'RED' USING A VARIETY OF OBJECTS
Equipment
Red car, crayon, bead, cup, blue book, green crayon, yellow cup

1   Will point to a *red car* when asked to.
2   Will point to a *red car* when presented with a blue book in the array, when asked.
3   Will point to a *red crayon* when asked, presented in an array with a blue book and a yellow cup.
4   Will point to a *red bead* when asked, presented in an array with a blue book, yellow cup and green crayon.
5   Will point to a *red cup* when presented with five items of different colours.

(As above for remaining colours.)

C   NAMING THE COLOUR 'RED' USING ONE TYPE OF OBJECT
1   Will name the colour *red* when asked to, when presented with a red block.
2   Will name the colour *red* when asked to, when presented with red and blue blocks.
3   Will name the colour *red* when asked to, when presented with yellow and blue blocks.
4   Will name the colour *red* when asked to, when presented with yellow and blue blocks in different positions.
5   Will name the colour *red* when asked to, when presented with yellow, blue and green blocks in different positions.
6   Will name the colour *red* when asked to, when presented with yellow, blue, green and white blocks, in different positions.
7   Will name the colour *red* when asked to, when presented with yellow, blue, green, white and black blocks in different positions.

(As above for remaining colours.)

D   NAMING THE COLOUR 'RED' USING A VARIETY OF OBJECTS
Equipment
6 objects in colours of red, blue, yellow, green, white, black
1   Will name a *red car* when asked.
2   Will name a *red car* when asked, when presented with a blue cup.
3   Will name a *red jumper* when asked, when presented in an array with a blue cup and a yellow crayon.
4   Will name a *red shoe* when asked, when presented in an array with a blue cup, yellow crayon and green bead, in different positions.
5   Will name a *red toothbrush* when asked, when presented with six or more objects of different colours.

(As above for remaining colours.)

The colour programme was carried out with a boy of six years, J.K. He was a boy with no speech, and a mental age of approximately one year. He was able to visually inspect and track. It was decided to teach him to attend to verbal instructions and focus on objects that he usually put in his mouth. To increase his level of 'understanding' was also felt to be desirable in this case, and colour was chosen as a target. Only the first two stages A and B of the programme of objectives were carried out.

An example of two weeks' recording follows. Five trials a day were allowed for each step of the programme.

Record sheet

Name: J.K.
Task: Will point to a red block with a blue, yellow and green in addition, when asked.
Step: 6

Criterion of success: 75%
Week number: 7

KEY
√ = completed/successful
o = attempted
x = no response

						Totals		
Trials	Mon.	Tues.	Wed.	Thurs.	Fri.	Success	Attempt	No resp.
1	o	o	o	o	√	1	4	–
2	√	√	√	o	√	4	1	–
3	o	o	√	√	o	2	3	–
4	√	√	√	√	√	4	–	–
5	o	√	o	o	o	1	4	–
					Grand totals	12	12	–

Percentages
completed/successful = 50%
attempted = 50%
no response = 0

Record sheet

Name: J.K.
Task: Will point to a red block with   *Criterion of success:* 75%
a blue, yellow and green in addition,   *Week number:* 12
when asked.
Step: 6

KEY
√ = completed/successful
o = attempted
x = no response

						Totals		
Trials	Mon.	Tues.	Wed.	Thurs.	Fri.	Success	Attempt	No resp.
1	√	√	√	√	√	5	–	–
2	o	o	o	√	√	2	3	–
3	√	o	√	o	o	2	3	–
4	o	√	o	√	√	3	2	–
5	√	√	√	o	o	3	2	–
					Grand totals	15	10	–

Percentages
completed/successful = 60%
attempted = 40%
no response = 0

A graphical respresentation of J.K.'s progress after fifteen weeks is presented in Fig. 12; after this it was decided to go on to another colour, 'blue'.

The results of J.K.'s progress with the colour blue after fourteen weeks is given in Fig. 13. Several objects were used to teach this colour as in stage 2, to prevent fixation on a single object.

Teacher's comments
J.K.'s teacher reported that she was pleasantly surprised at the boy's progress. J.K. had presented to her as a boy who had a fair receptive

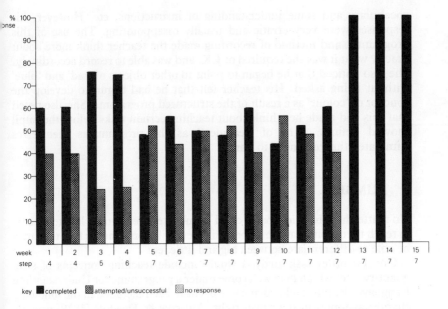

Fig. 12 Identifying the colour red by pointing: pupil J.K.

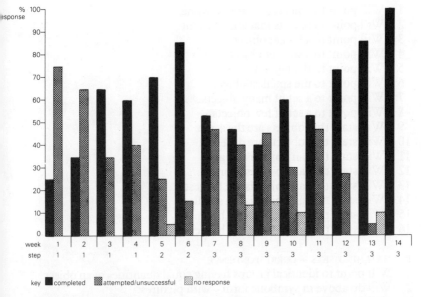

Fig. 13 Identifying the colour blue by pointing: pupil J.K.

vocabulary and some understanding of instructions, etc. However, his responses were very erratic and usually disappointing. The use of this programme and method of recording made the teacher think more about exactly what it was she required of J.K. and was able to record accordingly. She also noticed that he began to point to other objects of 'red' and 'blue' without being asked. His teacher felt that he had begun to develop the concept of 'colour' as a result of the structured programme. She also noted that this had made her think about teaching certain tasks before the pupil showed definite signs of 'readiness' as the programmes themselves stimulated the 'readiness' to learn.

B   NUMBER

No matter how handicapped a child is, most teachers would like to be able to teach them some early number skills, even if it only means that they may be able to differentiate between big and little, etc.

Our 1st order task analysis would include teaching concepts of size, quantity, etc. which may well come under a programme for Understanding Language. In this book, such concepts have been included in the following chapter as topics in their own right. Ainscow & Tweddle (1979) provide additional advice on this topic.

Objectives (1st order analysis)
A   LANGUAGE OF SIZE AND QUANTITY
1   Will point to objects that are the same.
2   Will point to objects that are different.
3   Will point to a longer object.
4   Will point to a shorter object.
5   Will point to the biggest object.
6   Will point to the smallest object.
7   Will point to a set of many objects.
8   Will point to a set of few objects.
9   Will state that objects are the same.
10   Will state that objects are different.
11   Will state that an object is longer.
12   Will state that an object is shorter.
13   Will state that an object is the biggest.
14   Will state that an object is the smallest.
15   Will state that a set of objects has many.
16   Will state that a set of objects has few.

B   MATCHING SETS − CORRESPONDENCE
1   Will point to identical groups having equal quantities of an object.
2   Will do above in symbolic form – with pictures.
3   Will underline groups of objects with equal quantities of the same

object.

4   As above with equal quantities of different objects.
5   Will draw in missing number of objects to make it equal to that of another set of objects.
6   Will construct equal sets of objects with bricks, etc.
7   Will state that two sets of objects are the same even though they are set in different spatial arrangements.

C   NUMBER
1   Repeats numbers from 1 to 10 after teacher, when teacher points to each in turn and says them.
2   Points to each number from 1 to 10 when asked to with physical prompt.
3   Writes each number from 1 to 10 by joining dots.
4   Writes each number from 1 to 10 by tracing it.
5   Completes each number from 1 to 10 begun by teacher.
6   Copies each number from 1 to 10.
7   Writes each number from 1 to 10 when called out.
8   Writes each number from 1 to 10 from memory.

(As above for numbers 10 to 20, etc.)

D   ADDITION − 1–10
1   Will add digits to make a total of 2 using abacus, counters or unifix blocks, when + sign is present.
2   Will do above when sum is written in both horizontal and vertical planes.
3   Will add digits to make a total of 3 using apparatus when + sign is present.
4   Will do above when sum is written in both horizontal and vertical planes.
5   Will add digits to make a total of 4 using apparatus, and when + sign is present.
6   Will do above when sum is written in both horizontal and vertical planes.
7   Will add digits to make total of 1, 2, 3 and 4 when + sign is present, using apparatus.
8   Will do above when sums are written in both horizontal and vertical planes.
9   Will add digits to make a total of 5, when + sign is present, using apparatus.
10 Will do above when sums are written in both horizontal and vertical planes.
11 Will add digits to make a total of 6, when + sign is present, using apparatus.
12 Will do above when sum is written in both horizontal and vertical planes.
13 Will add digits to make totals of 1, 2, 3, 4, 5 and 6 using apparatus.

14 Will do above when sums are written in both horizontal and vertical planes.
15 Will add digits to make a total of 7 when + sign is present, using apparatus when sums are written in horizontal and vertical planes.
16 Will do above to make a total of 8.
17 Will do above to make totals of 1 to 8.
18 Will do above to make a total of 9.
19 Will do above to make a total of 10.
20 Will do above to make totals of 1 to 10.

Note: It is usually the case that most E.S.N. (S) children will always need the help of some apparatus and therefore the programme has not included objectives for addition using no apparatus. However, if a child is able to do so then it should be included as a final stage in the programme.

Subtraction

A similar series of objectives can be written for this process, substituting the sign and wording appropriately.

Addition to 20

A similar series of objectives can be written for this goal, remembering to include the earlier learning of numbers 1 to 10, so as to prevent forgetting. This must also be done for numbers 11 to 15 when teaching numbers from 16 to 20, to prevent forgetting. It will also be necessary to include objectives which stipulate the way two digit numbers are to be written, for example, 'Will add two digit numbers to make a total of 16 using apparatus, with the tens and units written in the correct column.'

Record sheet

ADDITION

Task	Date started	Date achieved
Adds 1 + 1		
Adds to 3		
Adds to 4		
Adds to 5		
Adds to 6		
Adds to 7		
Adds to 8		
Adds to 9		
Adds to 10		
Adds 1 to 10		
Adds to 11		
Adds to 12		
Adds to 13		
Adds to 14		
Adds 15 + 16		
Adds to 17		
Adds to 18		
Adds to 19		
Adds to 20		
Adds 1 to 20		

C TELLING THE TIME

Being able to tell the time involves knowledge of certain concepts and
number value that the pupils may need to be taught in parallel. For
example, it may be part of a language programme to teach the concept of

'past', 'before', 'morning', 'afternoon', etc. The child must also be taught to recognize numbers and learn their value, which may be part of a number programme.

Techniques
Errorless discrimination learning
Prompting

Equipment
Large plastic clockface with movable hands
Small plastic clockface with movable hands
Mantelpiece/wall clock with numbers
Wristwatch with numbers
Clock stamp

Objectives
A   RECOGNITION OF NUMBERS AND HANDS
1   Will point to at least five different watches/clocks in an array of other objects when asked, 'Tell me which one tells the time.'
2   Will say 'watch'/'clock' when such an object is pointed to and child is asked, 'What is this?'
3   Will point to each number on the clockface beginning with the 1 and ending with 12, when each number is called out.
4   Will say the number on the clockface when it is pointed to, beginning with 1 and ending with 12.
5   Will point to each number on the clockface when called out in a random order.
6   Will say each number on the clockface when pointed to in a random order.
7   Will point to big hand with physical prompt when asked, 'Show me the big hand.'
8   As above with verbal prompt.
9   As above with no prompt.
10 Will point to the small hand with physical prompt when asked, 'Show me the small hand.'
11 As above with verbal prompt.
12 As above with no prompt.
13 Will point to the small hand with physical prompt in response to direction 'Show me the hand that tells the hour.'
14 As above with verbal prompt.
15 As above with no prompt.
16 Will say 'small hand' in response to question 'Which hand is this?'
17 Will point to the big hand with physical prompt in response to direction 'Show me the hand that tells the minutes.'
18 As above with verbal prompt.
19 As above with no prompt.

20   Will say 'big.hand' in response to question 'Which hand is this?'

B   TELLING TIME BY HOURS
  1   Will tell the time by the hour beginning at 1 o'clock, and ending at 12
        o'clock on a large plastic clockface.
  2   Will do above on a small plastic clockface.
  3   Will do above on wall clock.
  4   Will do above on wrist watch.
  5   Will tell time by the hour in a random order on large plastic clockface.
  6   As above on small plastic clockface.
  7   As above on wall clock.
  8   As above on wrist watch.
  9   Given a small plastic clockface, will move hands to indicate hours from
        1 to 12 o'clock.
 10   Given a small plastic clockface will move hands to indicate hours called
        out in a random order.

C   HALF HOURS
  1   Will say 'half past' when minute hand is on 6, when small hand is at
        every position from 1 to 12 in order.
  2   As above when small hand is moved randomly from 1 to 12.
  3   Will move hands on small plastic clockface to indicate 'half past' 1 to 12
        in order.
  4   As above in any order.

D   LEARNING 'PAST' AND 'TO'
  1   When minute hand is moved anywhere on the right hand side of
        clockface (1 to 6) will say 'past', when asked 'Is it "past" or "to"?' Every
        hour is covered in this way.
  2   When minute hand is moved anywhere on left side of clockface (6 to 12),
        will say 'to', when asked 'Is it "past" or "to"?' Every hour is covered in
        this way.
  3   Will correctly identify 'past' or 'to' when minute hand is moved
        randomly to cover every hour.

E   MINUTES
  1   Reads aloud minutes 'past' in 5's from 5 past to 30 minutes past, for
        every hour on small plastic clock.
  2   Reads aloud minutes 'to' in 5's from 25 minutes to 5 minutes to for every
        hour on a small plastic clock.
  3   Reads aloud minutes 'past' in 1's from 1 minute past to half past, for
        every hour on a small plastic clock.
  4   Reads aloud minutes 'to' in 1's from 29 minutes to to 1 minute to for
        every hour on a small plastic clock.
  5   As objective 1 with wrist watch.
  6   As objective 2 with wrist watch.

7   As objective 3 with wrist watch.
8   As objective 4 with wrist watch.

F   QUARTER HOURS
  1   Will point to a clockface in a book showing the big hand on the 3, when asked, 'Show me the face that tells quarter past', when in an array of two clockfaces showing different times, with physical prompt.
  2   As above with verbal prompt.
  3   As objective 1 with three faces in array.
  4   As objective 2 with three faces in array.
  5   As objective 1 with four faces in array.
  6   As objective 2 with four faces in array, etc.
  7   Will move hands on a plastic clockface to indicate quarter past every hour when asked for in order from 1 to 12.
  8   As above in random order.
  9   As objective 1 for 'quarter to'.
  10 As objective 2 for 'quarter to'.
  11 As objective 3 for 'quarter to'.
  12 As objective 4 for 'quarter to'.
  13 As objective 5 for 'quarter to'.
  14 As objective 6 for 'quarter to'.
  15 As objective 7 for 'quarter to'.
  16 As objective 8 for 'quarter to'.

G   TELLING TIME USING ALL THE PREVIOUS OBJECTIVES
  1   Will tell time correctly on a plastic clockface for:
      O'clock
      Half past
      Quarter past
      Quarter to
      Minutes past
      Minutes to
  2   As above on wrist watch.
  3   Will draw a big hand in correct place for stamped clockface for every hour written underneath, and for small hour in place.
  4   Will draw a small hand in correct place for every hour in a stamped clockface, with the hour written underneath for every hour.
  5   Will draw big hand in correct place for half hour times in stamped clockface when time is written underneath.
  6   As above for quarter past.
  7   As above for quarter to.
  8   As above for minutes past.
  9   As above for minutes to.

The above can be further broken down by the inclusion of dotted lines that the child joins; or a visual cue to indicate where their drawing should be.

Example of one record sheet

TELLING TIME BY HOURS

	Time	Large plastic clock	Small plastic clock	Wall clock	Wrist watch
I N O R D E R	1 o'clock				
	2 o'clock				
	3 o'clock				
	4 o'clock				
	5 o'clock				
	6 o'clock				
	7 o'clock				
	8 o'clock				
	9 o'clock				
	10 o'clock				
	11 o'clock				
	12 o'clock				
R A N D O M	5 o'clock				
	1 o'clock				
	7 o'clock				
	9 o'clock				
	11 o'clock				
	6 o'clock				
	3 o'clock				
	2 o'clock				
	4 o'clock				
	8 o'clock				
	10 o'clock				
	12 o'clock				

Note: The programmes in this section have been structured to prevent rigidity of learning which often happens if, for example, 'time' is only taught using plastic clockfaces as part of the classroom equipment. We are actually building transfer of training into our programmes. We are also making sure that the pupil not only learns by having to point or answer questions, but also has to actively show his or her learning, by moving clock hands, and working in a book.

D   CONCEPTS AND LANGUAGE OF TIME

In order that children can sequence events in time, they need to have some understanding of concepts that relate to the past, present and future. These include certain abstract concepts such as 'now', 'then', 'yesterday', and 'tomorrow'. Pupils will also require appropriate language for referring to particular units of time, for example, a day, a week, a month, a year etc. Knowledge of positional concepts would also be of importance, for example, 'first', 'second', 'last' etc. as they provide information about the ordering of events. In addition, concepts such as 'before', 'after', and 'next' should be part of any teaching programme on 'time'. Programmes relating to the concepts of time also involve auditory and visual sequential memory. Although the latter two abilities can be taught in isolation, as skills in their own right, they can be assimilated into the teaching of time to reinforce the notion of events following one another. A selection of programmes are presented in this section covering the understanding of past, present and future tenses; units of time; positions and sequential memory.

The pupils most likely to benefit from such programmes are those who may have the necessary vocabulary to refer to units of time etc., but who have difficulties in using such language in its proper context. As a result their verbalizations may make little sense, impairing their communication skills. Some children confuse past with future events and have little conception of how long certain units of time actually are. For instance, while a pupil may know that 'tomorrow' is in the future, he/she may be unsure as to how far into the future, and how long they have to wait until tomorrow arrives. Such pupils would also gain from experiencing some of these tasks.

Understanding of concepts relating to the past, present and future

Concepts to be taught:

Yesterday	Today
Last	Tomorrow
Ago	Then
Before	Now
Previously	Afterwards
Next	Later
Morning	Afternoon
Evening	Night

Techniques
Modelling
Shaping
Backward chaining

Equipment
A   Cards which tell stories through pictures:
   1 set of 2 picture cards of an event
   1 set of 3 picture cards of an event
   1 set of 4 picture cards of an event
   1 set of 6 picture cards of an event
These can include comic strip type events. Events should be chosen that depict the passing of time, from within a period of a few hours to days.

B   Tape recordings of events recounted verbally. These can vary with some events having two components only, for example, 'I got up; I went to school,' to those with four or six components, for example, 'My mum called me; I got out of bed; I ate my breakfast; I caught my bus.' The tapes should include words such as those given above as concepts you wish to teach. A further set of tape recordings should have certain of these concepts 'wiped off', so that pupils can insert them.

Objectives
A   USING PICTURE CARDS, REQUIRING VISUAL SEQUENCING
   1   Will place remaining picture in correct place (in set of two) when asked, 'Which one comes *before* this?' with a physical prompt.
   2   As above with a verbal prompt.
   3   Will do as above when asked, 'What happens before this?'
   4   Will place last picture in correct sequence (in a set of three) when asked, 'What comes *after* this?' when given a physical prompt.
   5   As above with a verbal prompt.
   6   Will place last two pictures in a set of three, when asked, 'What comes *after* this?' with a physical prompt.
   7   As above with a verbal prompt.
   8   Will place last two pictures in a set of three, when asked, 'What comes *next*?' with physical prompt.
   9   As above with a verbal prompt.
   10 Will place last picture in a set of four, when asked, 'What happens *after* this?' with a physical prompt.
   11 As above with a verbal prompt.
   12 Will place last two pictures in a set of four when asked, 'What happens *next*?' with a verbal prompt.
   13 Will place last three pictures in a set of four, when asked, 'Finish this story off by showing me what happens *next*.'
   14 Will order a set of four pictures to tell a story in correct time sequence, when presented in random order, and asked, 'Put these pictures to show me what happens *first*, *second*, *next* and *last*.'

15   Will place last two pictures in correct sequence in a set of six, when asked, 'What comes *after* this?' with a physical prompt.
16   Will do as above with a verbal prompt.
17   Will place last four pictures in correct order in a set of six, when asked, 'What comes *next*?' with a physical prompt.
18   As above with a verbal prompt.
19   Will place remaining five pictures in a set of six when asked, 'What happens *after* this?'
20   Will place correct pictures in relevant place when two pictures are placed in random with spaces in between, when asked, 'Put the rest of the pictures in the right place to show what happens *first*, then those that come *after*, ending up with the one that comes *after* all the others or *last*.'

Those children who have good speech can be made to tell the story as they perform the task, using the concepts above. With a different set/sets of pictures, other concepts can be taught such as 'yesterday', 'today', 'tomorrow', 'next week' etc. Obviously there would have to be some indication on the pictures that days are the unit of time. This could be done by using calendars in the pictures to represent the passing of days, as can be found in comic strips.

B   USING TAPE RECORDINGS, REQUIRING AUDITORY SEQUENCING
1   Will listen to a two-component recording and say what part of the day it takes place in, e.g. morning, evening etc., when given a verbal prompt.
2   Will listen to a three-component recording and say what part of the day it takes place in, with a verbal prompt.
3   Will listen to a tape of a four-component recording, and say what parts of the day each referred to, with verbal prompting.
4   Will listen to a tape of a six-component recording, and say which parts of the day each referred to, when presented in correct order from morning to night.
5   Will listen to a tape of a three-component recording and say which parts of the day each referred to when presented in random order, with a verbal prompt.
6   Will listen to a tape of a four-component recording and say which parts of the day they are referring to, when presented in random order, with verbal prompting.
7   Will listen to a tape of a six-component recording and say which parts of the day they are referring to, when presented in random order, with verbal prompting.
8   As above with no prompting.

To add variation and interest to this programme, children from within a group can be asked to mime certain actions that refer to parts of the day, or units of time, and other children can guess. Those pupils who mime can in addition be asked to give an account of what they are doing, and other children can then try to decide what passage of time they correspond to. One further extension to this scheme involves combining visual and auditory sequencing using pupils who mime and give a verbal account of their action. A group of pupils can be asked to act out a particular sequence of actions that may happen at different times of the day or week. The pupils who watch can be given the job of putting these actions in the correct order to make sense. For an event that takes place during a single day, a possible set of actions could involve getting out of bed, brushing one's teeth, catching a bus, arriving at school, settling down to work. For events that occur over the span of a week, the school timetable can be used for illustration, for example, the beginning of the week may be depicted by going swimming, and the end of the week by a trip to the shops. Those pupils who do the acting can be moved around to fit in with the 'audience' perceptions of the sequence of events. This concrete activity can be particularly helpful to pupils who have difficulty grappling with abstract concepts. Following the moving around of the actors, the sequence of events can be acted again, so provide pupils with feedback as to the success or otherwise of their actions.

C   USING TAPE RECORDINGS WHERE CONCEPTS INVOLVING TIME HAVE BEEN DELETED

For this task, pupils will also need some visual representation of the words that have been deleted. These can be written on large card, in the order to match the tape recordings, and also in random order.

1   Will choose correct word from list (in correct order) to be inserted into the tape recording to make sense, with a physical prompt.
2   As above with a verbal prompt.
3   Will repeat sentence with correct word included, with a verbal prompt.
4   Will choose two correct words from list (in correct order) to be inserted into the tape to make sense, with a physical prompt.
5   As above with a verbal prompt.
6   Will repeat sentence with correct word included, with a verbal prompt.
7   Will choose a three-word phrase from list (in correct order) to be inserted into the tape to make sense, with a physical prompt.
8   As above with a verbal prompt.
9   Will choose correct word from list (in random order) to be inserted into tape to make sense, with physical prompt.
10   As above with a verbal prompt.
11   Will repeat sentence with correct word inserted, with a verbal prompt.
12   Will choose two words from list (in random order) to be inserted into the tape recording to make sense, with a physical prompt.
13   As above with a verbal prompt.
14   Will choose three words from list (in random order) to be inserted into the tape recording to make sense, with a physical prompt.
15   As above with a verbal prompt.

Some pupils may recognize symbols more easily than words, and these can easily be substituted for words. Alternatively, other pupils can mime the words/symbols on the list, and those engaged on the programme can indicate their choice by pointing to one of their fellow pupils.

Understanding of length of time per unit, or between one unit and the next one

Equipment
Coloured markers (counters, cards, etc.)
Sticks, or spoons, etc. to make sounds with
Pictures of food depicting certain meals
Toothbrushes
Cards with the sun and moon drawn on them

The essence of the programme is that pupils can count out or 'mark' the number of meals, episodes of teeth cleaning, rising suns etc. before the next unit of time is reached.

Objectives
1 Will count out the correct number of meals (cards with pictures of food) to depict how 'long' it is until *tomorrow*, with a physical prompt and verbal cueing.
2 As above with verbal prompting.
3 Will count out the correct number of breakfasts to depict how long it is until *tomorrow*, with a physical prompt and verbal cueing.
4 As above with verbal prompting.
5 Will count out the correct number of teeth cleaning episodes to depict how long it is until *tomorrow*, with a physical prompt and verbal cueing.
6 As above with verbal prompting.
7 Will count out the number of rising suns there are until *next week*, with physical prompt and verbal cueing.
8 As above with verbal prompting.
9 Will tap out with stick the number of dinners until *next week*, with a physical prompt and verbal cueing.
10 As above with verbal prompting.
11 Will count out the number of moons there will be until a *fortnight* is reached, with physical prompting and verbal cueing.
12 As above with verbal prompting.
13 Will tap out with a stick how many days there are until the *end of the week* is reached, with physical prompting and verbal cueing.
14 As above with verbal prompting.
15 Will take away the number of meals (on card) to go back to *yesterday morning*, with physical prompt and verbal cueing.
16 As above with verbal prompting.

17   Will take away the number of rising suns to go back to *last Friday*, with physical prompting and verbal cueing.
18   As above with verbal prompting.
19   Will tap out the number of tea times it would take to go back to *two days ago*, with physical prompting and verbal cueing.
20   As above with verbal prompting.
21   Will count out the number of markers it takes to go back to *last month*, using days as the unit of time, with physical prompting and verbal cueing.
22   As above with verbal prompting.
23   Will use markers to count out the number of hours till the end of the school *day*, with physical prompting and verbal cueing.
24   Will tap out the number of tasks he/she has to do until *lunchtime* in school.
25   Will count out how many breakfasts there are until the *weekend* with physical prompting and verbal cueing.
26   As above with verbal prompting.

Similar objectives can be written for other combinations of time. Recording can be done easily on the standard sheet shown on page 15, so that each individual can achieve at his/her own pace and appropriate criterion level of success.

E   CONCEPTS OF SIZE, WEIGHT, LENGTH AND QUANTITY

Children with learning difficulties often fail to understand instructions because of poor conceptual development (McKinney 1972). They will therefore have great difficulties in understanding language and carrying out tasks. The teaching of concepts is very important and can be done in a structured and systematic fashion as shown by Clark (1971) and Becker *et al* (1971). Donaldson (1978) has shown that the manner in which a child is asked to perform tasks involving conceptual knowledge affects performance as do the objects they are asked to handle. The following programmes were constructed with these points in mind.

The programmes presented below refer to the concepts of size, length, weight and quantity. They were drawn up initially for a set of twins aged twelve years, T.C. and L.C. Both girls had severe learning difficulties and showed signs of disturbed behaviour. Although they did not respond to any formal testing, their teachers reported that they were fairly able children in tasks involving hand–eye co-ordination, receptive vocabulary and visual and auditory discrimination. Their self-help skills were adequate in that they were able to dress, feed and look after themselves with verbal prompting. The teachers of these twins wished to extend their performance in class. The twins could use two-word utterances but preferred to use non-verbal signals with adults and peers. The programme therefore had built into it the minimum of speech requirements, although the twins were always encouraged to verbalize. It was not, however, necessary for verbalizations to occur in order to succeed on the programme.

Note: While these programmes were drawn up with consideration being given to tasks progressing in order of difficulty, it was left to the discretion of the teacher to begin the sequence of activities at a point which seemed appropriate to her. As a result each teacher assessed the pupil to get a base line before beginning on the programme. For this reason some of the steps of the programmes were superfluous for the pupils and were omitted. The teachers also varied the order of the steps to introduce variety and to stimulate the pupils. Some steps were repeated at intervals throughout the operation of the programme to raise the level of success. Sometimes two or three steps of the programme were carried out in the same week as this was felt to be in the pupils' interest and within their ability. As the programmes were finely graded the teachers often found that a few steps could be merged into one as the pupils were more able than the programme anticipated. Objects and equipment were also changed to suit the preferences of the pupils who were very particular about what they would interact with in their environment. The availability of certain objects in the classroom also affected what was eventually used by the teachers.

Size

Aim: To discriminate large and small objects by giving; pointing; sorting; making; cutting/tearing; spinning top to indicate relevant word.

Objects

Beads	Buttons
Blocks	Dolls
Bottles	Sweets
Spoons	Plasticine
Cups	Food/food substitute
Books	

Facilitators
Flash cards with words 'big' and 'little'
Spinning top with slot

Techniques
Shaping
Errorless discrimination learning

Criterion of success
75% per objective

Objectives
1 Will match large plastic shapes.
2 Will match small plastic shapes.
3 Will match various shapes of paper cut outs.
4 Will give teacher *big* spoon with a big and a small spoon present.
5 As above in rotated positions.
6 Will give teacher a *big* bead with a big and a small bead present.
7 As above in rotated positions.
8 Will give teacher a *big* bottle with a big and a small bottle present.
9 Will give teacher a *small* block with a big and a small block present.
10 As above in rotated positions.
11 Will give teacher a *small* button with a big and a small button present.
12 As above in rotated positions.
13 Will give teacher a *big* bead with an assortment of big and small objects present.
14 Will give teacher a *small* cup with an assortment of big and small objects present.
15 Will sort out a group of similar coloured buttons into piles of 'big' and 'little'.
16 Will do above and place flash cards near appropriate piles.
17 Will sort out a group of buttons of two different colours into piles of 'big' and 'little'.
18 As above and will place flash cards near appropriate piles.
19 Will sort out a group of multi-coloured sweets into piles of 'big' and 'little', and place flash cards appropriately.
20 Will point to a *big* piece of cake when asked, presented with pieces of different sizes.
21 Will point to a *little* piece of cake when asked, presented with pieces of different sizes.
22 Will point to a *big* doll when asked, presented with two different sized dolls.
23 Will point to a *little* doll when presented with two different sized dolls.
24 Will make a *big* ball out of plasticine when asked after being shown how to do it.
25 Will make a *little* ball out of plasticine when asked.
26 Will make a *big* and *little* ball out of plasticine when asked.
27 Will spin top to indicate word 'big' when asked, 'Is this a big book or a little book?'
28 As above for cup.
29 As above for bottle.
30 As above for sweet.
31 Will spin the top to indicate word 'little' when asked to indicate the relative size of three different objects.
32 Will cut a *big* piece of cake when asked after being shown how to do it.
33 Will cut a *little* piece of cake when asked after being shown how to do it.
34 Will order a set of objects from big to little and vice versa.

The results of the programme for T.C. are shown in Fig. 14. L.C.'s results are indicated in Fig. 15. It can be seen that T.C. went through the programme in half the time it took her twin. She was also able to order objects in terms of size whereas L.C. did not achieve at all on that target. She was also more able to point to the words 'big' and 'little' reaching a higher level of success than L.C. A typical week's recording for L.C. can be seen below.

Note: The words 'little' and 'small' are used interchangeably.

Record sheet

Name: L.C.
Task: Concept of size
Step: Will make big balls of plasticine when asked.

Criterion of success: 75%
Week number: 7

KEY
$\sqrt{}$ = completed/successful
o = attempted
x = no response

| | | | | | | Totals | | |
Trials	Mon.	Tues.	Wed.	Thurs.	Fri.	Success	Attempt	No resp.
1	x	x	x	$\sqrt{}$	$\sqrt{}$	2	–	3
2	x	o	o	$\sqrt{}$	$\sqrt{}$	2	2	1
3	x	x	o	$\sqrt{}$	$\sqrt{}$	2	1	2
4	x	o	o	$\sqrt{}$	$\sqrt{}$	2	2	1
5	x	x	o	$\sqrt{}$	$\sqrt{}$	2	1	2
Grand totals						10	6	9

Percentages
completed/successful = 40%
attempted/unsuccessful = 24%
no response = 36%

Teacher's note: L.C. brought out the clay, emptied small pieces and rolled them into a ball. She said 'big ball' with no prompting.

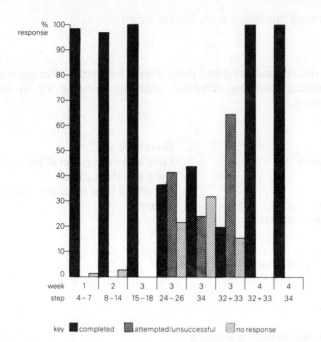

Fig. 14   Concept of size – big, small/little, bigger, smaller: pupil T.C.

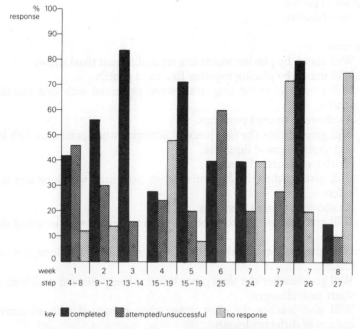

Fig. 15   Concept of size – big and little: pupil L.C.

Length

Aim: To discriminate long and short objects by giving; pointing; making; cutting/tearing; painting; drawing; ordering; spinning top to indicate relevant word.

Objects

Straws	Short tube of mints
Pipe cleaners	Long and short pieces of liquorice
Rulers	Long and short chains
Pencils	Pictures of long and short sticks of
Plasticine	lollipops
Long tube of smarties	

Facilitators
Flash cards with words 'long' and 'short'
Spinning top with slot

Techniques
Shaping
Errorless discrimination learning

Criterion of success
75% per objective

Objectives
1   Will match by placing together a set of different sized straws.
2   Will match by placing together like sized pencils.
3   Will give teacher the *long* straw when presented with long and short straws.
4   As above in rotated positions.
5   Will give teacher the *long* piece of liquorice when presented with long and short pieces of liquorice.
6   As above in rotated positions.
7   Will give teacher the *long* ruler when presented with long and short rulers.
8   As above in rotated positions.
9   Will give teacher the *short* pencil when presented with long and short pencils.
10   Will give teacher the *short* chain when presented with long and short chains.
11   Will give teacher the *short* pipe cleaner when presented with long and short pipe cleaners.
12   Will give teacher the *short* straw when presented with an array of objects of different length.
13   Will give teacher the *long* pencil when presented with an array of

objects of different length.
14   Will point to the *long* lollipops in the picture when presented with long and short pictures of lollipops.
15   Will point to the *short* lollipops in the picture when presented with long and short pictures of lollipops.
16   Will point to the word 'long' when presented with flash cards of 'long' and 'short'.
17   Will point to the word 'short' when presented with flash cards of the words 'long' and 'short'.
18   Will make a *long* sausage out of plasticine when asked (at least 12–15 cm).
19   Will make a *short* sausage out of plasticine when asked (between 5–8 cm).
20   Will make a *long* road out of smarties/mints when asked (at least 25 cm).
21   Will make a *short* road out of smarties/mints when asked (between 10–15 cm).
22   Will cut straws into *long* and *short* pieces.
23   Will cut pipe cleaners into *long* and *short* strips when asked.
24   Will draw a *long* line/man when modelled.
25   Will draw a *short* line/man when modelled.
26   Will spin top to indicate appropriate word in an array of long and short pencils.
27   As above with pencils and straws.
28   As above with chains, liquorice and pipe cleaners.
29   Will complete ordering of a set of straws by placing shortest in its correct position.
30   Will complete ordering of a set of liquorice by placing the medium sized piece in its correct position.
31   Will complete ordering of a set of pipe cleaners by placing the longest in its correct position.
32   Will order a set of three differing lengths of straws from longest to shortest.
33   Will order a set of four differing lengths of straws from longest to shortest.

The results of T.C.'s progress on this programme are presented in Fig. 16. She took about five weeks to complete the programme. It is evident that those parts of the programme involving T.C. cutting and drawing proved the most difficult as she had to show her understanding of the concepts at a higher order level than when giving or pointing. T.C. was allowed to tear paper instead of 'cut', as she had difficulty using scissors. Her twin L.C.'s results are given in Fig. 17. Once again she took almost half as much time again to complete the programme as T.C. She did not manage to do more difficult aspects of the task such as cutting.

A typical week's recording for T.C. can be seen on page 95.

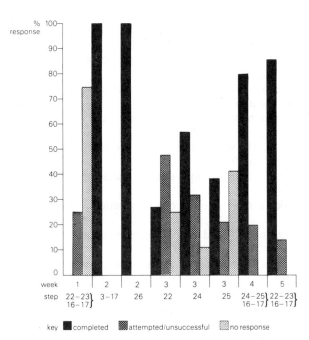

Fig. 16   Concept of length – long/short/longer/shorter: pupil T.C.

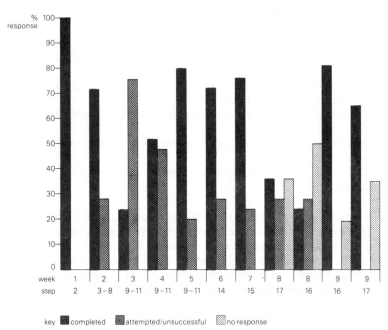

Fig. 17   Concept of length – long/short/longer/shorter: pupil L.C.

Record sheet

Name: T.C.
Task: Concept of length
Step: Will cut straws into long and
short lengths.

Criterion of success: 75%
Week number: 3

KEY
√ = completed/successful
o = attempted
x = no response

Totals

Trials	Mon.	Tues.	Wed.	Thurs.	Fri.	Success	Attempt	No resp.
1	x	x	√	√	x	2	–	3
2	x	x	o	√	x	1	1	3
3	x	x	√	o	x	1	1	3
4.	x	x	√	o	x	1	1	3
5	x	x	√	√	x	2	–	3
Grand totals						7	3	15

Percentages
completed/successful = 28%
attempted/unsuccessful = 12%
no response = 60%

Weight

Aim: To discriminate heavy and light objects by: filling bags; lifting
objects; spinning top to indicate relevant word; piling objects; ordering
objects.

Objects
Empty and full tin cans
Sand
Buckets/flower pots/yogurt cartons
Baskets
Books

Scrap paper
Full and empty jars (not transparent)

Facilitators
Flash cards with words 'heavy' and 'light'
Spinning top with slot

Techniques
Shaping

Criterion of success
75% per objective

Objectives
1   Will lift up an empty and a full tin can and give *heavy* one to teacher.
2   Will lift up an empty and a full tin can and give *light* one to teacher.
3   As above in rotated positions.
4   Will lift up two books of different weights (but of similar appearance) and give *heavy* one to teacher.
5   Will lift up two books of different weights (but of similar appearance) and give *light* one to teacher.
6   Will fill two identical yogurt cartons, one with sand and the other with scrap paper, and give *heavy* one to teacher.
7   Will fill two identical yogurt cartons, one with sand and the other with scrap paper, and give the *light* one to teacher.
8   Will make a *heavy* pile of objects when asked.
9   Will make a *light* pile of objects when asked.
10   Will make a *heavy* and a *light* pile of objects side by side when asked.
11   Will point to appropriate flash cards with word 'heavy' when asked.
12   As above with 'light'.
13   Will place flash cards alongside objects, e.g. full tin, empty bottle, etc.
14   Will complete an array of objects of differing weights by placing *lightest* in correct position.
15   Will complete an array of objects of differing weights by placing *heaviest* in correct position.
16   Will complete an array of objects of differing weights by placing the medium weight in correct position.
17   Will spin top to indicate correct word in an array of heavy and light objects for the word 'heavy'.
18   As above for the word 'light'.

T.C.'s progress on the programme is presented in Fig. 18. The teacher varied the sequence of steps, and often combined some as the very fine grading of steps was not found to be necessary for T.C. Some steps were repeated to raise the percentage level of success. In steps 14–16 the number of objects in an array was also varied, beginning with three objects and ending with a total of seven objects. These steps were also merged so that T.C. responded by placing objects to indicate both *heavy* and *light* in the same step. The programme took nine weeks to complete, and was terminated when T.C. was able to place an object in its correct position (in terms of weight) in an array of seven objects. At the time of writing, L.C. had not begun on this programme.

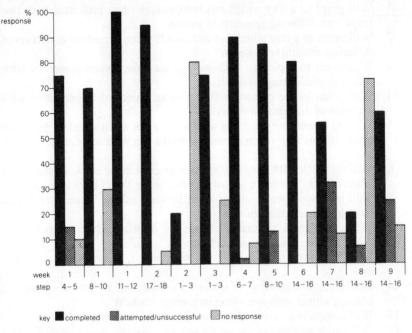

key ▪ completed ▨ attempted/unsuccessful ▧ no response

Fig. 18   Concept of weight – heavy/light: pupil T.C.

Quantity

Aim: To discriminate greater and lesser masses using the concept of 'more' and 'less' by: pointing; filling; spinning top to relevant word; making; ordering.

Objects
Bottles (identical but transparent)   Crisps
Plasticine   Drink child enjoys
Trays   Pictures of masses of objects
Sweets   Empty crisp bags

Facilitators
Flash cards with words 'more' and 'less'
Spinning top with slot

Techniques
Shaping

Criterion of success
75% per objective

Objectives
1 Will point to a tray which has *more* sweets when presented with two trays with differing amounts of sweets.
2 Will point to a tray which has *less* sweets when presented with trays of differing amounts of sweets.
3 Will point to a picture with *more* of an object when presented with pictures of differing amounts.
4 Will point to the picture with *less* of an object when presented with pictures of differing amounts.
5 Will fill one empty crisp bag with *more* crisps when asked to 'put more crisps in this bag' when presented with a bag with some crisps already in it.
6 Will fill bottle with *more* liquid when given another bottle a quarter full when asked, 'Put more squash in your bottle than I have in mine.'
7 Will take some water out of a bottle when asked, 'Make your bottle have *less* squash than mine.'
8 Will complete a picture of objects by drawing others around when asked, 'Make this picture have *more* . . . .'
9 Will cross out objects in a picture when asked, 'Make this picture have *less* . . . .'
10 Will complete an array of differing amounts of sweets on saucers by placing saucer with one sweet in correct position.
11 Will complete an array of sweets on saucers from *most* to *least*.
12 Will order an array of sweets on saucers, placing the one with the *most* sweets in its correct position.
13 Will place correct flash card near bottle with *more* water.
14 Will place correct flash card near bottle with *less* water.
15 Will spin top to indicate correct word in an array of *more* and *less* objects.
16 As above in rotated positions.

At the time of writing neither twin has progressed on to this programme on quantity.

Teacher's comments
T.C.'s teacher had taught T.C. for six years and had a close relationship with her. She had always felt that T.C. was far more able than she indicated and wanted to teach her something to stretch her, and prove that her responses were indicative of quick and efficient learning compared with the other children in her class. She felt that T.C. raced through these first three

programmes, and·was using the words 'big', 'little', 'long' and 'short' spontaneously. T.C.'s concentration span was noted to improve markedly and she would often request to do more work on the programme than was planned for any one day. For the first time T.C.'s teacher could show in concrete terms both how quickly and how well she consolidated information. T.C.'s teacher also mentioned that she became aware of the difference between saying that a child 'knew' something when the task merely involved pointing/giving, and actually showing knowledge by doing, for example, making, cutting, filling, etc. This made T.C.'s teacher less likely to feel disappointed if T.C. did not always perform according to plan, because it depended so much on what exactly she required T.C. to do in order to indicate mastery of a concept.

T.C.'s teacher retired halfway through the completion of the programmes. She had been very concerned about T.C.'s reaction to new members of staff, and whether or not her performance would deteriorate. In fact T.C. has had two new members of staff since, and each has been able to continue the programmes with the minimum of difficulty. The new teachers were grateful for the precise way in which the programmes were constructed, as this enabled them to carry on where the programmes had been left off quite easily.

L.C.'s teacher was not as optimistic as T.C.'s teacher about her ability to go through the programmes, especially those tasks which required her to identify words. This was borne out in some respects in that L.C. took much longer to reach the required criterion of success per objective, and her success rate per task was lower than that of her twin. However, L.C.'s teacher noticed that on those occasions when classroom factors prevented her from carrying out the programmes, L.C. would resent this and her behaviour would deteriorate. L.C.'s teacher felt that it was useful to record in such a detailed manner as it provided a very clear picture of L.C.'s learning pattern. This was especially helpful because L.C. was on medication and often had days when she would be particularly unresponsive and lethargic. L.C. was also in the habit of pinching herself, causing severe breaking and soreness of the skin. When she was working on the programme this behaviour lessened. Something particular to aim for with L.C. was found to be advantageous, so her disturbed behaviour could not always be used as an excuse for not doing a structured programme with her, or not following any specific schedule of activity.

10   Self-help skills

Children who have severe learning difficulties may achieve comparatively little in the cognitive area of development. However, they can and often do attain quite high levels of social, self-help and independence skills. Wilson (1981) stresses the importance of such skills in planning a curriculum for children in special schools.

The following are useful in planning programmes in the area of self-help skills: Kiernan & Jones (1977); Baker *et al* (1978); Burland *et al* (1977) and Kiernan *et al* (1978). Jeffree and Cheseldine (1982) provide a comprehensive check list of self-help and independence skills.

The programmes presented below are a selection of those constructed for pupils in a residential special school, at the request of the staff.

A   DRESSING

Putting on a nightdress

Techniques
Backward chaining
Physical prompting
Verbal prompting
Fading

Objectives
1   Will pull the hem of her nightdress down from her hips, while helper's hand holds hers, giving a physical prompt.
2   Will pull the hem of her nightdress down from her hips when helper places her hand on the gown saying, 'Pull your nightie down.'
3   Will pull the hem of her nightdress down from her waist when helper holds her hands, and does it with her.
4   Will pull the hem of her nightdress down from her waist when helper places her hands on the gown and says, 'Pull your nightie down.'
5   Will pull her nightdress down from her chest when helper holds her hands and does it with her.
6   Will pull her nightdress from her chest when helper places her hands on her gown and says, 'Pull your nightie down.'
7   Will pull her sleeves down from the elbows to the wrists when helper holds her hands and does it with her.
8   Will pull her sleeves down from the elbows to the wrists when helper places a hand on the sleeve and says, 'Pull your sleeve down.'

9   Will pull her sleeve down from her shoulders to the wrists when helper holds her hands and does it with her.
10 Will pull her sleeves down from the shoulders to the wrists when helper places a hand on the gown and says, 'Pull your sleeves down.'
11 Will place arms in armholes when helper holds gown ready, and pull nightdress own.
12 Will place arms in armholes when helper says, 'Put your arms in the armholes.'
13 Will pull nightdress down from face and complete process when helper places her hands on the gown.
14 Will pick up nightdress in the correct orientation (front/back) and complete process when helper says, 'Put your nightie on.'
15 Will pick up nightdress and turn it from front to back and complete process when helper says, 'Put your nightie on.'

The above programme was used with S.T., a twelve-year-old girl who was severely handicapped. She was ambulant, very active, but had no speech. While her class teacher concentrated on hand–eye co-ordination tasks, the residential care staff began the process of helping her achieve some self-help skills. Fig. 19 presents the results of S.T.'s progress on step 1 after twenty weeks. The first step was carried out for this length of time as a success rate of 75 per cent per step, per week was the initial target. However, this was reduced to a target of 60 per cent as it was felt that the first target was obviously unrealistic. In any event it showed just how long some handicapped children can take to achieve mastery of a small step within a programme.

It can be seen from Fig. 19 that for the first seven weeks S.T. showed little response, but after that began to make attempts and gradually perform the task although not to a high enough level to indicate mastery. An example of the recording from week seven to thirteen for S.T. on this programme is shown on page 103, all for step 1. Recordings from weeks number thirty-four to forty are shown on page 104, for step 2.

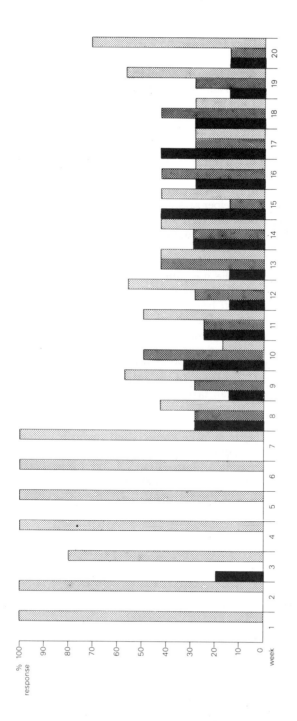

Fig. 19 Dressing – pulling hem of nightdress down from hips, with a physical prompt: pupil S.T.

Record sheet

Name: S.T. *Criterion of success:* 75% per week *Reward:* Sweet
Task: To pull hem of nightdress down from hip level with a physical prompt.

KEY
√ = successful
o = attempted
x = no response

Week	Step	Mon.	Tues.	Wed.	Thurs.	Fri.	Sat.	Sun.	Totals Succ.	Att.	N.R.	Percentages Succ.	Att.	N.R.
7	1	x	x	x	x	x	x	x	–	–	7	–	–	100
8	1	x	o	x	√	o	√	x	2	2	3	28.5	28.5	43
9	1	o	x	o	x	x	x	√	1	2	4	14.3	28.6	57.1
10	1	o	√	o	x	o	x	ILL	2	3	1	33.3	50	16.7
11	1	√	x	x	x	AWAY	AWAY	o	1	1	3	25	25	50
12	1	o	x	√	o	x	x	x	1	2	4	14.3	28.6	57.1
13	1	x	o	o	x	o	x	√	1	3	3	14.4	42.8	42.8

Record sheet

Name: S.T. *Criterion of success:* 75% per week *Reward:* Sweet
Task: To pull hem of nightdress down from hip level with a physical prompt.

KEY
√ = successful
o = attempted
x = no response

Week	Step	Mon.	Tues.	Wed.	Thurs.	Fri.	Sat.	Sun.	Totals			Percentages		
									Succ.	Att.	N.R.	Succ.	Att.	N.R.
34	2	x	x	x	x	x	x	x	–	–	7	–	–	100
35	2	o	o	x	x	x	x	o	–	3	4	–	43	57
36	2	x	x	√	x	x	√	o	2	1	4	29	14	57
37	2	o	√	√	√	ILL	ILL	ILL	3	1	–	75	25	–
38	2	x	√	√	ILL	ILL	ILL	ILL	2	–	1	67	–	33
39	2	ILL	ILL	ILL	√	x	ILL	ILL	1	–	1	50	–	50
40	2	ILL	√	ILL	ILL	ILL	ILL	ILL	1	–	–	100	–	–

Putting on a sock

Techniques
Backward chaining
Prompting
Fading

Objectives
1 Will pull up sock from ankle when sock has been put on as far as the ankle with a physical and verbal prompt.
2 Will pull up sock from toe when sock has been put on as far as the toe with a physical and verbal prompt.
3 Will place sock on toe and pull up with a verbal prompt.

The above programme was constructed for J.D., aged eight. This programme was used by the class teacher who wanted to put J.D.'s hand–eye skill to use by teaching her self-help skills. The results of the programme are presented in Fig. 20. It can be seen that on steps 1 and 2 J.D. achieved over 60 per cent success every week for the first six weeks, and indeed on weeks three, five and six reached 100 per cent success. When she was moved to step 3 her performance dropped dramatically. Between weeks seven and twelve she had four peaks of 'No response' at the 100 per cent level. After the twelfth week her level of 'Attempts' rose sharply and by the fifteenth week J.D. reached a 50 per cent level of success on step 3. This step required maximum self-help and is obviously the most difficult to achieve. After nineteen weeks, J.D.'s 'Attempts' were around the 100 per cent level, and it could be expected that with more time she would achieve at the 60 per cent or higher criterion of success.

Putting on a jumper

Techniques
Backward chaining
Prompting
Fading

Baseline
J.D. could already pull her jumper down from chest level.

Objectives
1 Will pull jumper down from neck level when jumper is placed over head and through arms.
2 Will place jumper over head and complete process when jumper is handed to her ready to put head in neck hole, with verbal prompt.
3 Will put on jumper without any help, when asked to.

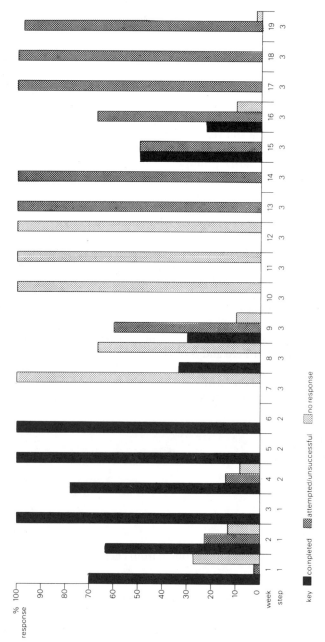

Fig. 20   Self-help – putting on a sock: pupil J.D.

The results of J.D.'s progress on this programme are shown in Fig. 21. It took four weeks for J.D. to achieve the target rate of 75 per cent success per step in a week for step 1. As soon as she was moved on to step 2 her level of success dropped to 20 per cent but by the ninth week she was achieving maximum success. Moving on to the final step reduced her level of successful performance to zero, but her level of attempts increased. By the thirteenth week J.D. began performing successfully to a level of 30 per cent and showed signs of continuing to achieve successfully, given more time.

It could be argued that the programme was not finely graded enough for this pupil. However, her teacher felt that she did not need the built-in reinforcement, and narrowed the skill down into the basic component parts.

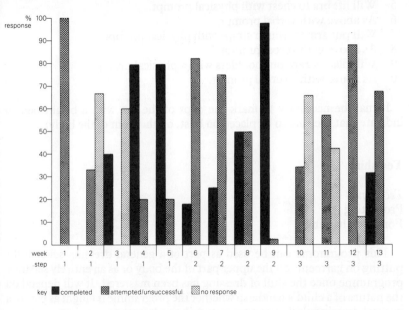

Fig. 21   Self-help – putting on a jumper: pupil J.D.

B   PUTTING ON CLOTHES THE CORRECT WAY AROUND

Many children with learning difficulties will have trouble with orientation, which can be seen when they try to put on their clothes the correct way around. Some common items are: bra, pants, tee shirt, jumper, dungarees, socks, shoes. For the purposes of illustration, the items 'bra' and 'tee shirt' are analysed below.

Bra

Techniques
Prompting
Forward chaining

Objectives (3rd order analysis)
1 Will fasten hooks in front of body at waist level with physical prompting.
2 As above with verbal prompting.
3 Will swivel hooks to back area with physical prompt.
4 As above with verbal prompt.
5 Will lift bra to chest with physical prompt.
6 As above with verbal prompt.
7 Will put arms through straps with physical prompt.
8 As above with verbal prompt.
9 Will place straps on shoulders with a physical prompt.
10 As above with a verbal prompt.

It may be necessary to mark the cups of the bra with a bright tag, to indicate that they are to be placed on bust, on the front of the body.

Tee shirt

Techniques
Prompting
Forward chaining

This programme can be used as part of a general dressing scheme for putting on garments on the upper part of the body or as an entirely separate programme once the skill of dressing has been mastered. It will depend on the nature of a child's handicap whether the programme is taught as part of a general dressing skill or as a separate task at a later date.

Objectives (3rd order analysis)
1 Will hold neck of tee shirt and 'point' to label or other conspicuous mark, e.g. child's own name, with adult pointing out label.
2 Will hold neck of tee shirt and point to label when given a verbal prompt.
3 Will turn neck of tee shirt around with the help of an adult so that the label is against chest.
4 Will turn neck of tee shirt around with the label against chest, with verbal prompt.
5 Will lift tee shirt in turned position over head and proceed to bring over head, with physical guidance.

6 Will lift tee shirt in turned position over head and proceed to bring over head, with a verbal prompt.
7 Will bring tee shirt over head to neck level, and look to see that no label/mark can be seen in the front, with physical guidance.
8 Will bring tee shirt over head to neck level and look to see that no label/mark can be seen in the front, with a verbal prompt.
9 Will proceed to complete the dressing process, with a verbal prompt.
10 If label is in front, will turn tee shirt around until no label can be seen, with armholes in correct position.

This programme can be shortened considerably for pupils needing less help, by beginning at step 8.

C   UNDRESSING

Taking off a jumper

Techniques
Backward chaining
Prompting

Objectives (3rd order analysis)
1 Will pull jumper over head when it is at eye level, with adult giving a physical prompt.
2 As above with verbal prompting
3 Will pull jumper over head when it is at chin level, with adult giving a physical prompt.
4 As above with a verbal prompt.
5 Will pull jumper off when at neck level with a physical prompt.
6 Will do as above with a verbal prompt.
7 Will take off jumper when arms have been taken out of sleeves to wrist level, with a physical prompt.
8 As above with a verbal prompt.
9 Will take off jumper when arms have been taken out of sleeves to elbow level, with a physical prompt.
10 As above with a verbal prompt.
11 Will take off jumper when arms have been taken out of sleeves at armpit level, with physical prompt.
12 As above with a verbal prompt.
13 Will remove arms from sleeves, with a verbal prompt.
14 Will remove jumper from chest level, with a physical prompt.
15 Will do above with a verbal prompt.
16 Will remove jumper from waist level, with a physical prompt.
17 As above with a verbal prompt.

18 Will remove jumper from hip level, with a physical prompt.
19 Will do above with a verbal prompt.

As it is unlikely that this type of programme is likely to be carried out several times a day, it is probably best to record when each step was begun and when achieved.

Sample record sheet

Name:
Task: Taking off a jumper   *Reinforcer:* Praise/physical contact

Step	Date started	Date achieved
1		
2		
3		
4		
5		
6		
7		
8		
9		
10		
11		
12		
13		
14		
15		
16		
17		
18		
19		

D   ENCOURÁGING DRESSING AND UNDRESSING

Some pupils who are used to being undressed and dressed fail to use skills they have probably acquired. In a residential special school it is possible to come across children who are somewhat institutionalized and need a tremendous amount of cajoling to become more self-reliant.

One such girl was L.R. She was thirteen years of age with Downs Syndrome. She responded well to drinks of coca-cola which were used as a reward in the following programme, carried out in an effort to motivate her to dress and undress herself with minimum verbal prompting. Morning and bed times were chosen as the appropriate time for monitoring the programme as these were the usual times for putting on and taking off clothes. The clothes involved were vest, pants, petticoat, skirt, jumper, dress/trousers, socks, shoes, nightdress and dressing gown.

The programme was carried out for eleven weeks, and the results are presented in Figs. 22 to 25 for the following articles of clothing: right shoe, skirt/dress, right sock and vest. A typical week's recording for the seventh week is shown on page 114. From the graphical representations of L.R.'s responses, it appears that while she seemed to put on her right shoe with relative ease, she experienced far less success with her right sock. The responses for putting on a dress/skirt and a vest both indicate erratic

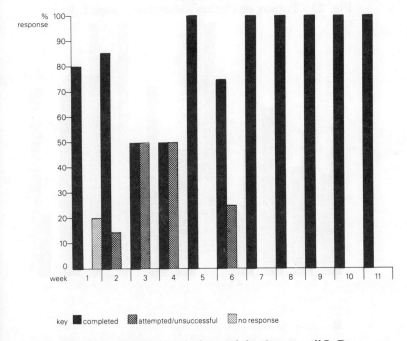

key ■ completed ▨ attempted/unsuccessful ▨ no response

Fig. 22   Putting on clothes – right shoe: pupil L.R.

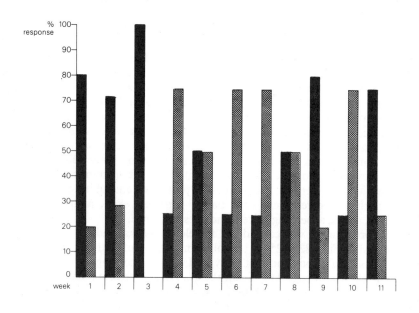

key ■ completed ▨ attempted/unsuccessful ▧ no response

Fig. 23 Putting on clothes – skirt/dress: pupil L.R.

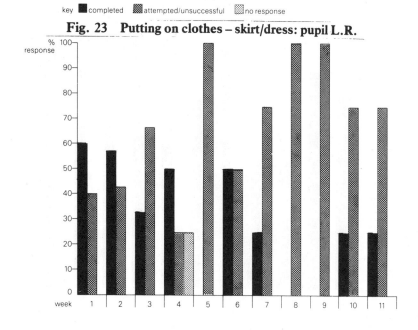

key ■ completed ▨ attempted/unsuccessful ▧ no response

Fig. 24 Putting on clothes – right sock: pupil L.R.

performances over the eleven weeks. However, this child had a greater success rate when putting on her vest than she did when putting on her skirt or dress. After the termination of the programme, L.R. was given some prompting for those articles of clothing that she seemed to dislike putting on, fading out the prompting for all the other articles, but giving her praise for the rest.

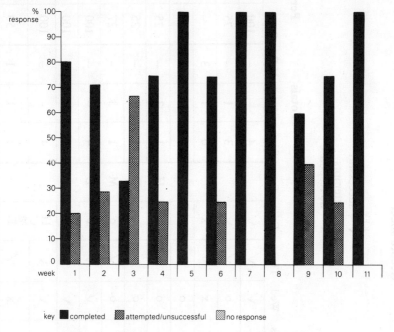

Fig. 25 Putting on clothes – vest: pupil L.R.

Record sheet

Name: L.R.
Week number: 7

KEY
√ = successful
o = attempts
x = no response

Clothes	Sun.	Mon.	Tues.	Wed.	Thurs.	Fri.	Sat.	Totals Succ.	Att.	N.R.	Percentages Succ.	Att.	N.R.
Vest			√	√	√	√		4	–	–	100	–	–
Pants			√	o	√	√		3	1	–	75	25	–
Petticoat			x	x	o	x		0	1	3	–	25	75
Skirt/jumper			x	o	o	√		1	2	1	25	50	25
Dress/trousers	H	H	o	o	o	√	H	1	3	1	25	50	25
Right sock	O	O	o	o	√	o	O	1	3	–	25	75	–
Left sock	M	M	o	o	√	o	M	1	3	–	27	75	–
Right shoe	E	E	√	√	√	√	E	4	–	–	100	75	–
Left shoe			√	√	√	√		4	–	–	100	–	–
Nightdress		√	√	√	√	H O M E		4	–	–	100	–	–
Nightgown		√	o	x	√	E		2	1	1	50	25	25

E   FEEDING

Using a spoon

The following programme was constructed for two pupils in a residential special school. They were assessed as in need of a structured approach for enabling them to use a spoon. One pupil, D.W., was a partially sighted girl of ten with severe learning difficulties. She used a specially adapted spoon. The other pupil was a severely handicapped girl of twelve, T.L., who had spent most of her life in a hospital setting. As part of the process of rehabilitation she was placed on self-help programmes of which feeding was one.

Techniques
Shaping
Backward chaining
Prompting
Fading

Objectives (3rd order analysis)
1   Will open mouth when loaded spoon touches lips and allow food to be placed in mouth.
2   Will open mouth when loaded spoon is 2 in.–4 in. away from mouth in anticipation and allow food to be placed in mouth.
3   Will hold helper's hand and raise loaded spoon to mouth when spoon is at child's chest level.
4   Will grip handle of spoon with helper's hand over child's hand when raised to chest level, and take to mouth.
5   Will grip handle of loaded spoon with helper's hand on top of child's hand when spoon is at elbow level, and take to mouth.
6   Will grip handle of loaded spoon with helper's hand on top of child's hand when spoon is raised just off the table (2 in.–4 in.) and take to mouth.
7   Will grip handle of loaded spoon when helper places child's hand on spoon and says, 'Take the spoon to your mouth.'
8   Will grip handle of spoon with helper's hand over child's hand, scoop food, and complete the feeding process.
9   Will grip handle of spoon and scoop food when helper says, 'Put some food on your spoon,' and complete the feeding process.
10 Will use spoon without any physical or verbal prompting.

Note: For some physically handicapped pupils additional steps may be needed to teach the gripping action, and to encourage reaching for a spoon. A frequency chart could be used to measure the number of times a pupil would reach for a spoon when held in front of him/her. In addition, if it is necessary to ensure that a child can grip and hold on to an object for a specified length of time, then a scheme could be operated where a variety of objects would be placed in the child's palm, and kept there for increasingly longer periods of time, for example, starting off with three seconds and graduating to thirty seconds.

The pupil D.W.'s results after seven weeks are presented in Fig. 26. She remained on the first step throughout to encourage overlearning and mastery before moving on to the next step.

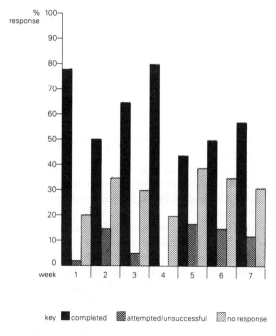

key ■ completed ▨ attempted/unsuccessful ▨ no response

Fig. 26   Feeding with a spoon: pupil D.W.

Fig. 27 shows the results of T.L.'s progress on step 9, which required her to scoop the food with the spoon unaided. Results after twelve weeks are shown on the chart. T.L. reached only 41 per cent success by the twelfth week. This was not felt to be at a sufficiently high level. She was therefore moved back to step 8 where she continued to have physical help with the scooping action, before going back to step 9. A typical week's recording for the seventh week is shown on page 118.

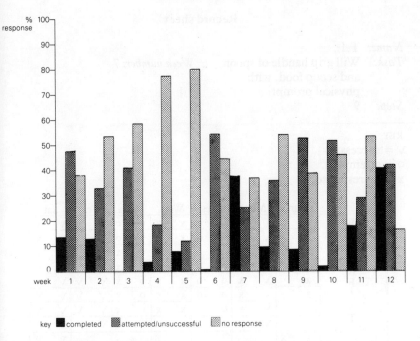

key ■ completed ▨ attempted/unsuccessful ▨ no response

Fig. 27   Feeding with a spoon – scooping action and completion of process: pupil T.L.

Record sheet

Name: T.L.
Task: Will grip handle of spoon   *Week number:* 7
and scoop food, with
physical prompt
Step: 9

KEY
√ = successful
o = attempted
x = no response

	Sun.		Mon.		Tues.		Wed.		Thurs.		Fri.		Sat.	
B	x	x	√	√	o	o	x	x	o	o	√	√	√	√
R	x	x	√	√	o	o	x	x	o	o	√	√	√	√
E	x		√	x	o	o	x	x	o	x	√	√	√	√
A	x		√	x	o	o	x	x	o	x	√	√	√	√
K	x		√	x	o	o	x	x	o	x	√	√	√	√
F	x		√	x	o	o	x	x	o	x	√	√	√	√
A	x		√	x	o	o	x	x	o	x	√	√	√	√
S														
T	x		√		o		x		o		√		√	
	x	x											√	√
	x	x	s		s		s		s		s		√	√
L	x		c		c		c		c		c		√	√
U	x		h		h		h		h		h		√	√
N	x		o		o		o		o		o		√	√
C	x		o		o		o		o		o		√	
H	x		l		l		l		l		l		√	
	x												√	
			o	o	o	o	x	x	x	x			o	√
			o	o	o	o	x	x	x	x			o	√
T	o		o	o	o	o	x	x	x	x	o		√	o
E	u		o	o	o	o	x	x	x	x	u		√	√
A	t		o	o	o	o	x	x.	x	x	t		√	√
			o	o	o	o	x	x	x	x			o	√
			o	o	o	o	x	x	x	x			√	√
			o		o		x		x				√	
Totals														
Succ.	–		10		–		–		–		15		41	
Att.	–		15		30		–		10		–		4	
N.R.	20		5		–		30		20		–		–	

Grand totals: successful   = 64   percentage = 32.3
attempted   = 59   percentage = 29.8
no response = 75   percentage = 37.9

F   TOILET TRAINING

There are two different types of programme in this area. One is to actually train the bladder and bowel control, and also to make the child more aware of his/her bodily functions. The second type of programme is for the slightly more able child who has 'accidents', and needs to be able to indicate his/her needs before the accident occurs. A useful text can be found in Azrin & Foxx (1978).

Rapid method

This involves collecting a baseline recording of the frequency of the child's wetting, soiling, and 'dry' periods. Once that has been done, the child is given frequent drinks to increase the likelihood of needing to use the toilet, so giving a greater opportunity for training.

A baseline should be recorded for between one and two weeks, depending on the child. It involves examining the child once every hour, and recording whether the child was wet, soiled or dry. A sample record sheet is given below.

Baseline recording for toileting

Name: *Week number:*   KEY W = wet
                                                    S = soiled
                                                    D = dry

Time	Mon.	Tues.	Wed.	Thurs.	Fri.	Sat.	Sun.
9.00							
10.00							
11.00							
12.00							
1.00							
2.00							
3.00							
4.00							

Totals   W =
             D =
             S =

The times when the examinations are made will vary according to whether they are being made during school hours or not. A record should be kept of the total number of 'wets', 'drys' and 'soiled' for each day. An average can then be calculated for each of these categories. This information will be useful when training the child to use the toilet in order to compare the child's performance before, during and after training.

Implementing the programme using the rapid toilet training method involves giving the child a drink every quarter hour or half hour, depending on how often the child will take a drink. The child must be placed on the toilet every half hour, and a record should then be kept of whether the child was wet when placed on the toilet, or whether he/she used the toilet. The child should be rewarded for sitting on the toilet, either with praise, music, affection, etc. There are special toilet 'chairs' on the market now which emit a musical tune when the child successfully uses it for urination/evacuation.

Non-rapid method

This method involves giving no extra drinks in between the child's usual drinking schedule. You attempt to train the child according to his/her pattern of wetting, as established when collecting baseline data. Following the collection of baseline data, the child should be examined every hour and taken to the toilet. If the child uses the toilet he/she is rewarded. However, with many children just sitting on the toilet is an achievement which should be recognized. A record of 'wets' and 'drys' needs to be kept so as to evaluate the programme.

Objectives (3rd order analysis)
The objectives are written in the order in which they are expected to be achieved, beginning with evacuating and ending with manipulation of clothes.

1 Will evacuate in toilet bowl when placed on toilet seat and held on seat until toileting is complete.
2 Will evacuate in toilet bowl when placed on toilet seat and given a verbal prompt.
3 Will sit on toilet for five seconds with physical and verbal prompting.
4 Will sit on toilet seat for ten seconds with physical and verbal prompting/praise.
5 Will sit on toilet seat for fifteen seconds with helper giving verbal prompting and playing musical instrument.
6 Will sit on toilet seat for twenty seconds with verbal praise only.
7 Will remove pants, with physical prompting, when facing toilet.
8 Will remove pants, with verbal prompting, when facing toilet.
9 Will undo zip, with physical prompting, when facing toilet.
10 Will undo zip, with verbal prompting, when facing toilet.

11 Will lift dress/skirt with physical help.
12 Will lift dress/skirt with verbal prompting.
13 Will indicate need by signing/saying 'toilet'.
14 Will indicate need by pointing to toilet.
15 Will indicate need by crying and holding self.
16 Will wipe self with toilet paper already broken off, with physical help.
17 As above with verbal prompting.
18 Will break off toilet paper with physical help and clean self.
19 As above with verbal prompting.
20 Will pull up pants with physical help.
21 Will pull up pants with verbal prompting.
22 Will pull down skirt/dress, *or* pull up trousers, with physical help.
23 As above with verbal prompting.
24 Will do up buttons/zip with physical guidance.
25 As above with verbal prompting.
26 Will flush toilet with physical guidance.
27 As above with verbal prompting.
28 Will wash hands with a physical prompt.
29 As above with verbal guidance.

It is sometimes felt that boys should be taught to use the toilet in the standing position. In this case, a judgement needs to be made about the level of a child's handicap, as to when that stage should be trained. Obviously, physically handicapped pupils may never achieve that state, or with developmentally young children this may be taught after the above sequence of steps has been mastered. The individual child's needs should allow for flexibility in the sequencing of objectives.

Sample record sheet for rapid toilet training

Name: *Week:*   KEY W = wet
                                                           D = dry
                                                           S = soiled

Time of drink	Mon.	Tues.	Wed.	Thurs.	Fri.	Sat.	Sun.
9.15							
9.30							
9.45							
10.00							
10.15							
10.30							
10.45							
11.00							
11.15							
11.30							
11.45							
12.00							
12.15							
12.30							
12.45							
1.00							
1.15							
1.30							
1.45							
2.00							

Totals: W =
              D =
              S =

G   BRUSHING TEETH

Techniques
Backward chaining
Shaping
Prompting and fading
Modelling

Objectives (3rd order analysis)
1   Will open mouth and hold helper's hand while helper brushes child's teeth.
2   Will spit out toothpaste when given verbal prompt.
3   Will open mouth and take the loaded toothbrush to mouth with physical guidance.
4   As above with verbal prompt.
5   Will take toothbrush to mouth and make two up and down strokes on front teeth with physical guidance.
6   As above with verbal prompting.
7   Will take toothbrush to mouth and make four up and down strokes on front teeth with physical guidance.
8   As above with verbal prompt.
9   Will take toothbrush and make six up and down strokes with physical prompt.
10   As above with verbal prompt.
11   Will take toothbrush to mouth and make four side to side brush strokes on side teeth with physical guidance.
12   As above with verbal prompt.
13   Will take toothbrush to mouth and make forward and backward strokes on molars, both lower and upper on each side of mouth, with physical guidance.
14   As above with verbal prompting.
15   Will make six to eight strokes of all types to cover all teeth, with a physical prompt.
16   As above with verbal prompting.
17   Will spit out residue of toothpaste, with verbal prompting.
18   Will rinse out mouth, with a physical prompt.
19   As above with verbal prompting.
20   Will squeeze toothpaste on to brush with physical guidance.
21   As above with verbal prompt.
22   Will undo cap of tube of toothpaste with verbal prompt.
23   Will rinse out brush under tap with physical guidance.
24   As above with verbal prompt.
25   Will replace cap on tube of toothpaste with verbal prompt.

Sometimes the use of a mirror can provide useful feedback to a pupil on the effectiveness and accuracy of his/her actions on this task.

11   Skills of independence

In the senior sections of special schools, pupils are likely to be prepared to take part in community life by learning how to use public transport, cross roads, shop and recognize 'social' signs. They would also be learning how to become as self-sufficient as possible. This would involve learning the skills of cooking, using household gadgets, laundry, cleaning, bedmaking, using the telephone and handling money. For helpful texts see Jeffree & Cheseldine (1982) and Burland *et al* (1977).

A   DOMESTIC SKILLS

The following analysis provides a guide as to how the tasks in this area can be broken down into separate sections, and ways in which pupils can be taught to perform the tasks. A selection of these skills is further analysed into teaching objectives. The order in which these skills are taught will depend very much on the level of ability displayed by individual pupils, and their living circumstances. No special order is suggested in this breakdown.

Household tasks

Preparation:	Recognition:
Beverages	Kettle
	Taps
	Larder
	Tea, coffee, etc.
	Fridge
	Milk
	Tea pot
	Crockery
Snacks	Larder
	Tin opener
	Specified food items
	Cooker
	Cooking implements
	Saucepans/frying pans
	Cooking fats

Laundering	Washing machine
	Sink
	Taps
	Soap
	Switches
	Clothes
Cleaning	Broom
	Dustpan and brush
	Vacuum cleaner
	Switches
	Dustbins
	Duster
	Polish
	Dishcloth
	Cream cleansers

Taking 'Recognition', the following objectives can be written for recognition of cutlery and cooker parts.

Recognition of cutlery

Techniques
Errorless discrimination learning
Modelling
Prompting
Shaping

Item
Fork

Objectives (3rd order analysis)
1 Will point to fork when teacher takes pupil's hand to fork, saying 'fork'. No other items are present.
2 Will point to fork when given a physical prompt, with no other items present.
3 Will point to fork when given a verbal prompt, with no other items present.
4 Will point to fork with physical prompt, with a spoon present.
5 Will point to fork with a verbal prompt, with a spoon present in reversed positions.
6 Will point to fork with a physical prompt, with a spoon and knife present.
7 Will point to a fork with a verbal prompt, with a spoon and knife present in different positions.
8 Will point to a fork on command with three other items of cutlery present.

Similar steps can be written for other items of cutlery. After three items are recognized to criterion level, a final objective should be written to ensure that previously taught items have not been forgotten and that the pupil can correctly discriminate each item on request, for example:

Will point to knife, spoon, and fork on request when all are present.

If it is important that a pupil learns to distinguish different types of knives, then a similar set of objectives can be written.

Items
Table knife
Carving knife
Bread knife
Vegetable knife

1 Will point to carving knife, with physical guidance, with a table knife present.
2 Will point to carving knife, with a verbal prompt, with a table knife present.
3 Will point to carving knife, with physical prompt, when a table knife and bread knife are present.
4 Will point to carving knife, with a verbal prompt, when a table knife and bread knife are present.
5 Will point to carving knife, with physical prompt, when all other knives are present.
6 Will point to carving knife, with a verbal prompt, when all other knives are present.

Obviously discrimination of types of knives in isolation is not of any particular use. It would be advantageous to teach the pupil what the knives are used for. Associative/functional learning could be achieved by having actual food items and/or pictures of them so that pupils can place the correct knife by the type of food it is normally used with. Objectives can be written thus:

Functional learning: varying knives

Objectives
1 Will place bread knife by a loaf of bread when teacher guides pupil's hand, with no other knives present.
2 As above with verbal prompt.
3 Will place bread knife by a loaf of bread, with a physical prompt, with a vegetable knife present.
4 As above with a verbal prompt.

5 Will place bread knife by a loaf of bread, with a physical prompt, when a vegetable and table knife are present.
6 As above with a verbal prompt.

The remaining items can be taught in a similar manner. The first step where modelling is used should emphasize that pupils must grip knives by their handles.

Functional learning: varying food items and knives

Objectives
1 Will place vegetable knife by a vegetable, with physical guidance, when a table knife and bread knife are present.
2 As above with physical prompt.
3 As above with a verbal prompt.
4 Will place vegetable knife by a vegetable, with a physical prompt, when a table and bread knife are present, together with bread and butter present.
5 As above with verbal prompt.

This process can be repeated for all items, before the final objectives are taught.

6 Will place bread knife by bread when three other food items and three other knives are present.
7 Will place table knife by butter when three other food items and three other knives are present.
8 Will place vegetable knife by vegetables when three other food items and three other knives are present.

Recognition and use of cooker

Techniques
Modelling
Prompting
Shaping

Objectives (3rd order analysis)
1 Will point to mains switch when teacher takes pupil's hand to switch.
2 Will point to mains switch when asked.
3 Will put on mains switch in imitation.
4 Will put on mains switch when asked.
5 Will turn correct knob to put on bottom left hotplate with physical guidance.
6 As above with physical prompt.
7 As above with verbal prompt.

8   Will switch off bottom left hotplate with physical guidance.

9   As above with physical guidance.

10   As above with verbal prompt.

11   Will switch on bottom left hotplate when pointed to, with verbal prompt.

12   Will switch on bottom right hotplate when pointed to, with verbal prompt.

13   Will switch on top left hotplate when pointed to, with verbal prompt.

14   Will switch on top right hotplate when pointed to, with verbal prompt.

(As above for switching off.)

Recognition of other hotplates can be taught in a similar manner, as can recognition and operation of the grill.

With more able children who are able to recognize numbers and/or read the time, the use of the oven can be taught.

15   Will switch on oven to required temperature when teacher takes pupil's hand and executes task.

16   Will switch on oven to required temperature with a physical prompt, given the temperature on a card to work from.

17   As above with verbal prompt.

18   Will switch on oven on request without a written model of the temperature.

Recognition and use of cleaning implements

Techniques
Errorless discrimination learning
Modelling
Prompting
Shaping

Items

Washing-up brush	Furniture polish
Sponge	Dustpan and brush
Dishcloth	Pan scourer
Soap pad	Duster
Mop	Broom

Objectives

1   Will point to washing-up brush when given physical prompt and asked, 'What do we use to clean the dishes?' The pupil should be shown a picture of sink and dishes, or referred to an actual sink of dirty dishes.

2   As above with verbal prompt.

3   Will point to washing-up brush when given physical prompt and asked, 'Which one do we use to clean the dishes?' Pupil should be given a mop to discriminate from.
4   As above with verbal prompt.
5   Will point to washing-up brush when given a physical prompt and asked, 'Which one do we use to wash the dishes?' Pupil should be given a mop and a dustpan to discriminate from.
6   As above with verbal prompt.

The remaining items can be taught in similar ways, before teaching cleaning skills themselves.

Cleaning skills: use of broom

Techniques
Modelling
Shaping
Prompting

Objectives (3rd order analysis)
1   Will grip handle of broom when teacher takes pupil's hands and places them on broom.
2   Will extend broom in front and away from body with teacher giving physical guidance.
3   As above with verbal prompt.
4   Will bring broom towards self in sweeping action with physical guidance.
5   As above with verbal prompt.
6   Will make second sweeping motion towards self with a physical prompt.
7   As above with a verbal prompt.
8   Will make third sweeping motion towards self at a sixty degrees angle from left, with physical prompt.
9   As above with verbal prompt.
10 Will make fourth sweeping motion towards self but at a sixty degrees angle from right, with a physical prompt.
11 Will make six sweeping actions from centre left and right with verbal prompt.
12 Will bring debris together in a small pile (8 in. radius) with several small sweeping actions, given physical guidance.
13 As above with verbal prompting.

The next stage would involve teaching the use of the dustpan and brush, and sequencing that skill on to the use of the broom.

Cleaning skills: use of dustpan

Objectives
1 Will grip handle of dustpan in left hand with physical guidance, and hold the brush in the right hand. (For right handed pupils.)
2 As above with a verbal prompt.
3 Will place dustpan near debris tilting handle end upwards, with physical prompt, and sweep debris into pan with right hand.
4 As above with verbal prompt.
5 Will continue sweeping motion until all debris is in pan, with physical prompt.
6 As above with verbal prompt.

Making snacks

Techniques
Modelling
Shaping
Prompting

SANDWICHES
Objectives (3rd order analysis)
1 Will point to bread bin with physical guidance.
2 As above with a verbal prompt.
3 Will open bread bin with a physical prompt.
4 As above with a verbal prompt.
5 Will take out two slices of bread with a physical prompt.
6 As above with a verbal prompt.
7 Will close bread bin with a verbal prompt.
8 Will get butter from refrigerator/larder with a verbal prompt.
9 Will get a table knife with a verbal prompt.
10 Will spread butter on one side of each slice of bread after demonstration, with physical guidance.
11 As above with verbal prompting.
12 Will get required filling with physical prompting.
13 As above with verbal prompting.
14 Will spread filling on one slice of buttered bread with physical guidance.
15 As above with verbal prompting.
16 Will place second buttered slice of bread on filling with physical guidance.
17 As above with verbal prompt.
18 Will cut sandwich in half with physical guidance.
19 As above with verbal prompt.
20 Will carry out entire task with verbal prompting.

21 Will make a sandwich on request.

Other such tasks can be analysed and taught in similar ways. A set of possible objectives for making other snacks and one beverage is given below. Some series of objectives have a greater amount of guidance built in than others. Teachers can choose which suit particular individuals within their sphere and work accordingly.

BEANS ON TOAST
Objectives
1 Will get tin of beans from cupboard.
2 Will get a small saucepan.
3 Will switch on mains switch of cooker. (Adapt for gas.)
4 Will switch on hotplate/or light burner.
5 Will open tin of beans with tin opener.
6 Will place contents in saucepan and place saucepan on hotplate.
7 Will get spoon and stir beans.
8 Will get one slice of bread from a loaf.
9 Will place on grill tray (or toaster).
10 Will switch on/light grill or put on toaster.
11 Will watch toast and turn bread over appropriately.
12 Will remove toast when done, and place on a plate.
13 Will place hot beans on toast with a spoon.
14 Will turn off hotplate and grill.

BEEFBURGERS IN A BUN (from frozen state, or fresh)
Objectives
1 Will take beefburgers out of the freezer or refrigerator, with a physical prompt.
2 Will take out a frying pan from the cupboard, and place it on a hotplate on the cooker, with a physical prompt and verbal cueing.
3 Will take oil from cupboard, or fat from refrigerator, and place a small amount in the frying pan, with a physical prompt.
4 As above with a verbal prompt only.
5 Will put on main cooker switch, and put on the correct hotplate, with verbal prompt. (If gas is used, change wording accordingly.)
6 Will wait for the fat to heat, and turn down hotplate temperature with physical guidance.
7 As above with verbal prompting.
8 Will place one/two beefburgers in pan with a spatula/fish slice with physical guidance.
9 As above with verbal prompting.
10 Will allow beefburgers to cook on one side for two to three minutes, and then turn them over using a fish slice, with physical guidance.
11 As above with verbal prompting.
12 Will allow beefburgers to cook on other side for a few minutes and then

      lift them out of the fat with fish slice, and place them on a piece of kitchen paper to drain, with physical guidance.

13   As above with verbal prompting, including switching off the hotplate.
14   Will take a bread roll/bun and split it in half with a bread knife, with physical guidance.
15   As above with verbal prompting.
16   Will butter each side of the roll (if required) with a verbal prompt.
17   Will place a beefburger inside the roll with physical guidance.
18   As above with verbal prompting.
19   Will execute entire task with verbal cueing.
20   Will execute entire task with no prompting or cueing.

Beefburgers can also be grilled, and teachers who would wish pupils to be familiar with that technique could substitute grill for hotplate, missing out steps 3 and 6.

PREPARING SOUP USING TINNED SOUPS
Objectives
1   Will select a particular flavour/type of soup, e.g. vegetable, chicken etc. correctly with the help of a physical prompt.
2   As above with a verbal prompt.
3   Will open the tin with a tin opener with physical guidance.
4   As above with a verbal prompt.
5   Will take out a small saucepan from the cupboard and place it on a hotplate. Will empty contents of the tin into a saucepan.
6   As above with a verbal prompt.
7   Will empty the contents of the tin into the saucepan, with the help of a spoon, and physical guidance.
8   As above with a verbal prompt.
9   Will turn on hotplate switch, or light burner if gas is used, with physical guidance.
10   As above with a verbal prompt.
11   Will regulate temperature of hotplate with physical guidance, after task is modelled for pupil.
12   As above with a verbal prompt.
13   Will stir soup in saucepan with a wooden spoon with physical help.
14   As above with verbal prompting.
15   Will stop stirring the soup when bubbles appear on the surface when prompted by verbal cues.
16   Will turn off hotplate with verbal prompting.
17   Will pour the soup into a bowl with physical guidance.
18   As above with a verbal prompt.
19   Will execute entire task with verbal cueing only.
20   Will execute entire task with no prompting or cueing.

MAKING TEA

The following objectives assume the use of an electric kettle. Where kettle is placed on stove, alter wording appropriately.

Objectives
1 Will remove lead from electric kettle.
2 Will remove lid from kettle.
3 Will fill kettle from cold tap.
4 Will replace lid on kettle.
5 Will replace lead on kettle.
6 Will switch kettle on.
7 Will get milk from refrigerator.
8 Will get out teapot and cup and saucer.
9 Will pour a little milk into the cup.
10 Will switch off kettle when it has boiled.
11 Will put teabags in teapot.
12 Will put boiling water in teapot.
13 Will stir water in teapot.
14 Will pour tea into cups.

Recording for these household tasks can be done using the standard record sheets given on page 15, so that the pupil's attempts can also be monitored, and relevant criterion levels set for completion of the task. A master sheet on Independence Skills is given at the end of the chapter where terminal objectives can be plotted to give an overview of all independence acquired by a pupil.

B SHOPPING

This is a highly complex task involving the combination of several separate skills. These include recognition, identification, choice making, communicating, using money, queuing, and packing goods.

Most of these skills can be taught in the classroom first and then generalized to the shop setting. Errorless discrimination learning is the best way of teaching identification and recognition skills. They can be broken down as follows:

Packaging	*Food item*	*Brand*
Tin	Beans	X
Packet	Cereal	Y
Box	Eggs	Z
Bottle	Squash	T
Carton	Milk	U
Frozen packs	Vegetables	F
Tubs	Yogurt	G

The objectives for identification and recognition could be written thus:

Identification and recognition

Objectives (3rd order analysis)
1   Will pick out a tin with a verbal prompt when a bottle is present.
2   Will pick out a tin with a verbal prompt with a bottle and carton present.
3   Will pick out a tin with a verbal prompt when a bottle, carton and tub are present.
4   Will pick out a tin with a verbal prompt with four other packages present.

Other packages can be taught in similar ways using verbal prompts and reinforcements after every attempt. Actual food items meaningful to the pupil can also be taught in this manner.

Next, the pupil should be able to identify foods in a shop.

1   Will pick out a tin of beans from provision sections of a shop with a physical prompt.
2   As above with a verbal prompt.
3   As above on request.
4   Will pick out a packet of cereal from the cereal section of a shop with a physical prompt.
5   As above with a verbal prompt.

(Similarly for other items, and/or brands.)

Choice making or selection depends on the pupil's conceptual knowledge. For instance, the pupil needs to be able to pick out objects by size and colour. Those two concepts need to be taught prior to teaching the selection of items in a shop. After that one can teach selection in terms of size, colour and quantity.

Selecting items

Technique
Errorless discrimination learning, varying colour and size.

Objectives
1   Will pick out large green tin of cat food from an array of two large tins of cat food with different coloured labels.
2   Will pick out large green-labelled tin of cat food from an array of three large, differently labelled tins.
3   Will pick out large green-labelled tin of cat food from an array of six large, differently labelled tins.

4 Will pick out small red-labelled tin of cat food from an array of large and small tins of cat food with various coloured labels.
5 Will pick out a large yellow-labelled tin and a small blue-labelled tin of cat food from an assorted array.

Prompting here would be necessary for the more severely handicapped pupils. It will certainly be needed for all pupils in the shop setting.

The communicating part of the programme assumes that either the pupil has speech and can make his/her wishes known or that he/she carries a note of the intended purchases. A list of common phrases is helpful to teach the pupil, for example:

I would like a pound of . . . . . .
Please may I have six . . . . . . ?
Can I have a bar of chocolate?
Can I have a pint of milk?

These can be taught using modelling, where pupils repeat teacher's phrase with the appropriate items as references. Backward chaining can also be used where a pupil is required to complete a phrase, for example:
1 I would like a pound of apples.
2 I would like a pound of . . . . . .
3 I would like . . . . . .
4 I would . . . . . .
5 I . . . . . .
6 . . . . . .

Most schools will operate simulated shopping exercises where pupils practise going to ask for items, use money, etc. This is very valuable, but does not necessarily generalize to the real setting. It is essential that wherever possible pupils practise in real shops, perhaps beginning with newsagents for chocolate etc., before graduating to small shops and supermarkets.

The use of money is covered in the next section. Once it has been taught to the required level, the whole shopping process can be rehearsed as a skill in its own right.

C USING MONEY

Obtaining goods and services for themselves with money is an important part of the pupils' steps to independence. Some pupils may be able to recognize and identify coins and notes correctly, but not handle money with any ability when it comes to adding, subtracting, getting or giving change. Obviously a pupil's knowledge of number, and his/her ability to compute addition and subtraction problems will determine whether or not they are placed on a programme for handling money. For the purposes of this programme, it will be assumed that pupils can identify numbers, colours, shapes, and be able to add and subtract tens and units.

Recognition and use of money

Objectives (1st order analysis)
1   Can point to/give a 1p coin.
2   Can point to/give a 2p coin.
3   Can point to/give a ½p coin.
4   Can point to/give a 5p coin.
5   Can point to/give a 10p coin.
6   Can point to/give a 20p coin.
7   Can point to/give a 50p coin.
8   Can point to/give a £1 coin.
9   Can point to/give £1 note.
10 Can point to/give £5 note.
11 Can point to/give £10 note.
12 Can make up sums of money amounting to 5p, 10p, 15p, 20p, 25p, 30p etc.
13 Can make up sums of money amounting to 2p, 4p, 6p, 8p, 10p, 12p, 14p etc.
14 Can make up sums of money on request from a variety of coins.
15 Can give change for sums up to 10p, 20p, 50p, 75p, £1.
16 Can give change for up to £1, in 2p, 5p, 1p, 20p etc. pieces.
17 Can count on from a number to be able to check own change.

Recognition of coins

Techniques
Errorless discrimination learning
Modelling
Shaping
Prompting and Fading

Equipment
Paper coins and notes from games, e.g. Monopoly
Real coins and notes

Objectives (3rd order analysis)
These objectives are written assuming that paper coins are used to teach identification, before moving on to real coins. However, because many children may have problems in transferring their skill from paper coins to real ones, it is recommended that children are taught using real coins wherever possible.

1   Can point to/give a 1p coin with a physical prompt, after a demonstration, with no other coins present.
2   As above with a verbal prompt.
3   Can point to/give a ½p coin with a physical prompt, after a demonstration, with no other coins present.
4   As above with a verbal prompt.
5   Can point to/give a 1p coin with a verbal prompt, with a ½p coin present.
6   Can point to/give a ½p coin, with a verbal prompt, with a 1p coin present.
7   Can point to/give a 2p coin with a physical prompt, with no other coins present.
8   As above with a verbal prompt.
9   Can point to/give a 2p coin with a verbal prompt with a ½p and 1p coin present.
10 Can point to/give a 5p coin with a physical prompt, with no other coins present.
11 As above with a verbal prompt.
12 Can point to/give a 5p coin with a verbal prompt, when ½p, 1p, and 2p coins are also present.
13 Can point to/give a 10p coin with a physical prompt when no other coins are present.
14 As above with a verbal prompt.
15 Can point to/give a 10p coin with a physical prompt when ½p, 1p, 2p, and 5p coins are present.
16 Can point to/give a 20p coin with a physical prompt when no other coins are present.
17 Can do above with a verbal prompt.
18 Can point to/give a 20p coin with a verbal prompt when ½p, 1p, 2p, 5p, and 10p coins are present.
19 Can point to/give a 50p coin with a physical prompt, when no other coins are present.
20 Can do above with a verbal prompt.
21 Can point to/give a 50p coin with a verbal prompt when ½p, 1p, 2p, 5p, 10p and 20p coins are present.
22 Can point to/give a £1 coin with physical prompt when no other coins are present.
23 As above with a verbal prompt.
24 Can point to/give a £1 coin when all the other coins are present, given a verbal prompt only.
25 Can identify any coin on request by giving or pointing with no cues.

Occasionally pupils can only identify coins provided they are presented with the number uppermost. If they can turn over coins to find out what the number is, this is not too much of a handicap. However, children with the most severe learning problems may not do this, and additional objectives may have to be included in the list to take account of this. An example is given below:

1   Can point to/give a 1p coin when side with number on it is uppermost, with a physical prompt, after a demonstration, with no other coins present.
2   Can point to/give a 1p coin when side without number on it is upper-most, with a physical prompt, after a demonstration, with no other coins present.
3   Can point to/give a 1p coin when either side of the coin is uppermost, with a physical prompt, after a demonstration, with no other coins present.
4   Can point to/give a 1p coin when side with number on it is uppermost, with verbal prompt, with no other coins present.
5   Can point to/give 1p coin when side without number is uppermost, with a verbal prompt, with no other coins present.
6   Can point to/give a 1p coin, when either side of the coin is presented, with verbal prompt, with no other coins present.
7   Can point to/give a 1p coin, with side with number uppermost, with a physical prompt, when a ½p coin is present.
8   Can point to/give a 1p coin, when number side is not uppermost, with a verbal prompt, when a ½p coin is present.

Similar objectives can be written to take into account all the other combinations as given in the previous section. Objectives for the recognition of notes should follow a similar format.

Addition, subtraction, and change, using coins

Technqiues
Modelling
Prompting
Fading

Equipment
Paper coins
Real coins

Objectives (3rd order analysis)
1   Can make up the sum of 1p using ½p pieces with a physical prompt, following a demonstration.
2   As above with a verbal prompt.
3   Can make up the sum of 2p using 1p pieces with a physical prompt, following a demonstration.
4   As above with a verbal prompt.

5   Can make up the sum of 2p using 1p and ½p pieces with a verbal prompt, after a demonstration.
6   Can make up the sum of 3p using 2p, 1p and ½p pieces with a physical prompt and following a demonstration.
7   As above with a verbal prompt.
8   Can make up the sum of 4p using 1p, 2p and ½p pieces, after a demonstration, and with a physical prompt.
9   As above with a verbal prompt.
10 Can make up the sum of 5p using 2p, 1p and ½p pieces following a model, and with a physical prompt.
11 Can make up the sum of 6p using 2p, 1p, 5p and ½p coins following a model, with the help of a physical and verbal prompt.
12 Can make up the sum of 7p using 5p, 2p, 1p and ½p pieces following a demonstration, with prompting.
13 Can make up the sum of 8p using 2p, 5p, 1p and ½p pieces, with verbal and physical prompting.
14 Can make up the sum of 9p using 5p, 2p, 1p and ½p pieces, with verbal and physical prompting.
15 Can make up the sum of 10p using 5p, 2p, 1p and ½p pieces, with physical and verbal prompting.

These steps may need to be broken down further if a pupil continues to experience difficulty in making up sums of money with a variety of sets of coins. However, once they have witnessed the activity being carried out a few times, as in steps 1–12, the demonstration and modelling can be faded out in favour of prompting only. Some pupils may be able to make up a sum of money using only a certain combination of coins, and in these cases, it may be helpful to break down the steps to even smaller components. An illustration is given below:

MAKING UP THE SUM OF 10p USING A COMBINATION OF COINS
1   Can make up the sum of 10p, using two 5p coins, using physical prompting, following a demonstration.
2   As above with a verbal prompt.
3   Can make up the sum of 10p using five 2p coins, with physical prompting, after task has been modelled.
4   As above with verbal prompting.
5   Can make up the sum of 10p using ten 1p coins, with physical prompting, after the task has been demonstrated.
6   As above with verbal prompting.
7   Can make up the sum of 10p using twenty ½p coins, with physical prompting, after the task has been modelled.
8   As above with verbal prompting.
9   Can make up the sum of 10p, using one 5p coin, two 2p coins, and one 1p coin, with prompting.
10 Can make up the sum of 10p using one 5p coin, one 2p coin, two 1p

coins, and two ½p coins, with prompting, after a demonstration.

Sums greater than 10p can be taught in a similar fashion and then made more meaningful by using sums of money that pupils are likely to have to deal with in their everyday life, for example, for bus fare, chocolate bar, cassette, bag of crisps, magazine, canned drink, etc. This could be built into the shopping programme at a suitable point in time, with simulation exercises carried out in the school setting, before trying the skills out in a shop or on public transport. One example may be the purchase of a canned drink that may cost 34p. The following may be a way of training pupils to make up that sum of money from a pile of mixed coins:

PURCHASE OF A CANNED DRINK COSTING 34p
1   Will pick out a 20p piece and add to it a 10p piece, together with two 2p pieces, after a demonstration and prompting.
2   As above with a verbal prompt only.
3   Will pick out two 10p pieces and add to it two 5p pieces, with four 1p pieces, after a model and with prompting.
4   Will pick out one 10p piece, and add to it two 5p pieces, as well as four 2p pieces, three 1p pieces, and six ½p pieces, with modelling and prompting.
5   Will do as above with verbal prompting only.

Giving and checking change

This skill can best be taught by role playing buying/selling exercises. Allow the child to act as a shopkeeper in perhaps a newsagent's, where a variety of articles can be bought. Have ready some of the following objects:

Pen	Note book
Eraser	Sweet
Bag of crisps	Magazine
Chocolate bar	Pile of loose change
Greetings cards	

For sums up to 10p in value:
1   Will give change of 4p, using two 2p coins, when asked to sell a pen worth 6p, with the help of physical prompting.
2   As above with the help of verbal prompting, by aiding the pupil to count on from 4 until 10 is reached.
3   Will give change for a sweet costing 2p, using a 5p piece, a 2p piece, and a 1p piece, with a physical prompt.
4   As above with a verbal prompt.
5   Will give change for two items costing 8½p, e.g. eraser and sweet, by using a ½p coin and a 1p piece, with physical prompting.

6   As above with verbal prompting.

For sums of up to 50p in value:

1   Will give change for items costing 23p by using a 2p coin, a 5p coin and
    two 10p coins (or a 20p piece), with a physical prompt.
2   As above with a verbal prompt involving counting on from 23 to 50.
3   Will give change for items costing 36½p by using a ½p coin, a 1p coin, a
    2p coin, and a 10p piece (or two 5p pieces), with a physical prompt.
4   As above with a verbal prompt, counting on from 36½ to 50.
5   Will give change for items costing 11p by using two 2p coins, a 5p coin, a
    20p coin (or two 10p pieces) and a 10p piece (or one 5p piece and five 1p
    pieces) with physical prompting.
6   As above with verbal prompting.
7   Will give change for any amount up to 50p, with non-verbal signals to
    reinforce pupil, e.g. nod of head, smiles etc.
8   As above with no cues whatsoever.

For sums of up to £1 in value:

1   Will give change for items costing 69p by using a 1p coin and three 10p
    pieces (or one 10p piece and four 5p pieces; one 20p piece and one 10p
    piece etc.) with a physical prompt.
2   Will give change for items costing 69p, by using any of the combinations
    of coins above with a verbal prompt, by counting forward from 69 to
    100.
3   Will give change for items costing 81p by using two 2p pieces, one 5p
    piece, and one 10p piece (or four 1p pieces, five 2p pieces and one 5p
    piece) with physical prompt, by counting on from 81 to 100.
4   As above with a verbal prompt, by counting on from 81 to 100.

Objectives for any other amount can be written in a similar fashion. For
those children who are checking as opposed to giving change, the wording
can be conveniently altered from 'will give ......' to 'will count on from
......'. The items used for the role play exercises in shopping could be
used as reinforcers during these sessions for children who are achieving the
targets set for them.

D   USING THE TELEPHONE

Making and receiving telephone calls is a very necessary part of the social
and independence skills that young adults need to acquire if they are to take
their place in the community and communicate with people when distance
prevents them from doing so face to face. Many youngsters may have
telephones in their homes, but their level of skill in using the phone may be
limited. Some children may simply be able to recognize the ringing of the

phone, and be able to lift the receiver, but lack the conversation skills necessary to communicate effectively. Others may well be able to handle receiving a call, but not make calls themselves. The following series of objectives provides a list of skills pupils will need to use the phone, whether to make or receive a call. Following that list, objectives for the teaching of making and receiving a call are dealt with. There will obviously be some overlap between the two, especially when considering the conversation skills that are needed for both tasks. However, for the sake of clarity each is presented separately. As this skill involves many other sub-skills taught in other parts of the teaching scheme, they are referred to, but not broken down into fine detail. For instance, the recognition of number for dialling is not covered as that is contained in the section on Number (page 74).

Using a telephone

Objectives (1st order analysis)
1   Recognizes public phones.
2   Recognizes private phones (knowledge of colour and positioning is implicit here).
3   Lifts up receiver and places correct part to ear and mouth.
4   Selects correct numbers.
5   Dials numbers in correct sequence.
6   Can wait to speak until ringing has stopped.
7   Makes self known before starting conversation.
8   Asks for person for whom call is intended.
9   Can speak at appropriate time.
10   Can wait for an answer.
11   Can give a reply where necessary.
12   Can take/give a message.
13   Can wait for conversation to come to an end before putting receiver down.
14   Can say goodbye at appropriate time.
15   Can dial if engaged tone is present.
16   Can put right coin in public box where appropriate.

The latter two objectives can be placed elsewhere in the sequence of objectives, as they may have to be tackled several times before the child is successful in reaching a person by phone, when lines are busy.

With the variety of telephone systems currently available, use can be made of them for children who may have particular difficulties in dialling either for reasons of visual impairment or immobility of fingers. Therefore, push button systems, or those with sounds associated with each number, may be of immense value. Although the text refers mainly to dialling, substitute push button etc. where applicable. Internal telephones in school are ideal for beginning the teaching process, followed by private lines, for example, in pupils' own homes.

Making a telephone call

Techniques
Modelling
Shaping
Prompting
Fading
Forward chaining
Backward chaining

Equipment
Internal telephone system $\Big\}$ push button
External telephone system and dial
Public call box

A   USING BACKWARD CHAINING, MODELLING AND SHAPING TECHNIQUES
Begin with internal telephone system, followed by external systems.

1   Will say 'Hello' in imitation after the call has been dialled and the recipient of the call reached, with a verbal prompt.

2   Will hold receiver to ear, with physical guidance, and wait to listen for the phone to stop ringing, before saying 'Hello' with a verbal and physical prompt.

3   Will dial last number in imitation, with physical guidance, and complete process as outlined in steps above.

4   Will dial last number in imitation, with verbal prompt, and complete the process outlined above.

5   Will dial the last two numbers with a physical prompt and complete the process outlined above.

6   Will dial the last two numbers with a verbal prompt, and complete the process as outlined above.

7   Will dial the last three numbers with a physical prompt, and complete the process outlined above.

8   Will dial the last three numbers with a verbal prompt, and complete the process as outlined above.

9   Will dial the last four numbers with a physical prompt, and complete the process outlined above.

10   Will dial the last four numbers with a verbal prompt, and complete the process as outlined above.

11   Will dial the last five numbers with a physical prompt, and complete the process outlined above.

12   Will dial the last five numbers with a verbal prompt, and complete the process as outlined above.

13   Will dial a six-figure number with a physical prompt, and complete the process.

14   Will dial a six-figure number with a verbal prompt, and complete the process outlined above.

15   Will lift receiver off the hook with physical guidance, and place near one ear, listening for a dialling tone.
16   Will lift receiver off the hook, with a verbal prompt, and place near one ear, listening for a dialling tone.
17   Will identify a phone with physical guidance, in imitation.
18   Will identify a phone with verbal prompting.

The above sequence of steps is suitable for use with a pupil who may need maximum help in this task. For those who may need less help, and can learn at a slightly faster pace, the more usual forward chaining technique, which is presented below, can be used.

B   USING FORWARD CHAINING, MODELLING, AND SHAPING
1   Will identify a phone with physical guidance, by going towards a phone, or pointing to one.
2   Will identify a phone with a verbal prompt.
3   Will lift the receiver off the hook with physical guidance and modelling.
4   Will lift the receiver off the hook with a verbal prompt only and place correct part of receiver to ear, and mouthpiece to mouth.
5   Will dial first number in imitation, with physical guidance.
6   Will dial first number in imitation, with a verbal prompt only.
7   Will dial first two numbers in imitation, with physical prompt.
8   Will dial first two numbers in imitation, with a verbal prompt.
9   Will dial the first three numbers with a physical prompt.
10   Will dial the first three numbers with a verbal prompt.
11   Will dial the first four numbers with a physical prompt.
12   Will dial the first four numbers with a verbal prompt.
13   Will dial the first five numbers with a physical prompt.
14   Will dial the first five numbers with a verbal prompt.
15   Will dial a six-figure number in the correct order with a physical prompt and a *visual cue* of the numbers written down for reference.
16   Will dial a six-figure number in the correct order with a verbal prompt and a *visual cue* of the numbers written down for reference.
17   Will dial a six-figure number with the visual cue only, when asked.
18   Will dial a six-figure number in the correct order by finding the number in a personal directory or other reference point.
19   Will be able to recall own telephone number (if appropriate) and dial home when requested by staff.

C   SPEAKING ON THE TELEPHONE
Technique
Forward chaining

Objectives
1   Will say 'Hello' in imitation, when given a physical and verbal prompt.
2   Will answer a question using such words as 'yes', 'no' etc. when given a physical prompt and demonstration.
3   Will answer a question using appropriate words when given a verbal cue and prompt.
4   Will ask for person for whom call is intended by name in imitation, with verbal prompting, e.g. 'Please can I speak to . . . .'
5   Will leave message for the person for whom the call was intended if unable to speak to him/her immediately, by following demonstration of adult.
6   Will do as above with verbal cueing only.
7   If person is contacted, will say own name and give brief details of message, following demonstration.
8   Will do as above, with verbal cues only.
9   Will wait for a reply before continuing, with the help of a physical prompt.
10 Will wait for a reply before continuing with the help of minimal gestures only, e.g. nod of head to go on, etc.
11 Will make some verbal response to a statement or question directed at him/her immediately, without pausing for long periods of time, with the help of physical and verbal prompts, e.g. a touch on the arm to indicate time for response, and a model of response like, 'Say "Yes, I liked that part of the shop".'
12 Can initiate conversation by using a demonstration sentence, with a physical cue as to when to do so.
13 As above with a verbal cue only.
14 Can respond to the speaker giving signs with tone of voice as if to end conversations, by using physical cues and verbal models.
15 As above with physical prompt only.
16 Can end a conversation by him/herself, when given a physical prompt.
17 Can end a conversation by him/herself when given a verbal cue.
18 Can do above by using appropriate words, e.g. 'I have to go now', 'Goodbye' etc. when given a physical prompt.
19 Can say 'Goodbye' in response to speaker doing so, with a physical prompt.
20 As above with a verbal prompt.
21 Can place receiver down after saying 'Goodbye' once in response, or after the speaker has said 'Goodbye' in response to pupil, with a physical prompt and/or demonstration.
22 As above with a verbal prompt.

Additional objectives for those who are adept at this skill can include what to do if there is a bad connection, or if the pupil cannot hear/ understand the speaker on the other end of the line:

1 Will inform person to whom call is being made that pupil wishes to put the phone down and dial again.
2 Will put down phone and begin process again, with a verbal prompt.
3 Will ring operator to ask for a connection if unable to get it by direct dialling, with a physical prompt.
4 Will do above with a verbal prompt.
5 Will request person on the receiving end of the call to return the call if it is not possible to ring again, with physical prompt.
6 Will do as above with a verbal prompt.

D MAKING EMERGENCY CALLS
Techniques
Modelling
Shaping
Prompting
Fading

Objectives
1 Will identify the figures 999 as the emergency number in an array with one other three-figure number, given physical prompt.
2 Will identify the figures 999 as the emergency number in an array with one other three-figure number, given a verbal prompt.
3 Will identify the figures 999 as the emergency number in an array with two other three-figure numbers, given a physical prompt.
4 Will identify the figures 999 as the emergency number in an array with two other three-figure numbers, given a verbal prompt.
5 Will dial the correct number of digits in imitation, given a physical prompt.
6 As above with a verbal prompt.
7 Will wait for the phone to stop ringing before speaking, given a physical prompt.
8 As above with a verbal prompt.
9 Will listen for voice to say, 'Emergency services, which service do you require?', given a physical prompt.
10 As above with a verbal prompt.
11 Will give the name of the relevant service as soon as the voice has finished enquiring which service is required, with a physical prompt and demonstration.
12 As above with a verbal prompt.
13 As above with a verbal prompt only.
14 As above on request.

All programmes given for use of the telephone can be taught as part of a planned schedule in a school, if other members of staff can be relied on to assist in being on the receiving end. In addition it would also be useful if members of staff could make calls to pupils on both the internal system and an outside line, pretending to be particular persons, and request pupils to undertake messages as part of their learning. Parents could be asked to play their part in this exercise, by agreeing to make a call to either their own child or another pupil, to assist them in practising skills of receiving calls.

The use of a tape recorder could aid the learning process, by allowing practice of listening to a person speaking, without the benefit of watching them at the same time. Pupils could learn when to interject, and to anticipate changes in tone of voice and rate of speech, which would enable them to pace their contribution more effectively. A tape recorder could also reproduce model questions and answers, depicting particular types of conversation.

Children could play the tape over and over again if they wished to learn a special type of greeting, how to ask particular questions, and how to give and take messages. In addition, tape recordings of pupils' attempts at telephone conversations could provide feedback for them. They could then make the necessary changes in their communication skills on the telephone as a result. Games where taped conversations were used to predict what type of communication was going on would be useful for children in terms of learning to predict and anticipate different outcomes for conversations. The tape could be stopped at points, and pupils could be asked to suggest what the next person in the conversation could or should say to achieve a certain outcome.

Some children will need visual and auditory cues in order to maintain a telephone conversation, without long pauses between contributions. A system of lights turning on to indicate when it is their turn to speak would be helpful. A torch, or coloured light bulbs set to go on and off at appropriate times could add information for the pupil, for example, a red light may be an indication to stop and listen to the other person, whereas a green light would mean that it is your turn to speak, or 'speak now'.

Recording the progress a pupil has made on making a telephone call and beginning a conversation could be done using the standard record sheet on page 15. However, the number of trials may be reduced to as few as one or two a day. This type of recording would provide information about the attempts made by a pupil, so that the teacher could continue to work on a particular step of the programme until the criterion of success set for the pupil has been reached. Alternatively, if it is felt that a pupil is likely to learn the skills of making telephone calls relatively easily and quickly, a record sheet such as that given on page 148 can be used. Each part of the skill can be tested on internal, private and public telephone systems to ensure that a pupil has mastered the skill and can transfer it to any type of system.

Sample record sheet for making telephone calls

Step	Internal phone	Private phone	Public phone box
Identifies phone.			
Lifts receiver.			
Places earpiece to ear, and mouthpiece to mouth.			
Dials 1st number with prompt.			
Dials 2nd number with prompt.			
Dials 3rd number with prompt.			
Dials 4th number with prompt.			
Dials 5th number with prompt.			
Dials 6th number with prompt.			
Dials all numbers with prompt in correct order.			
Dials all numbers with no prompt.			
Gives name.			
Asks for person.			
Begins conversation.			
Waits for a reply.			

Receiving a telephone call

Objectives (1st order analysis)
1   Recognizes ringing of a telephone bell.
2   Approaches the telephone and lifts receiver off the cradle.
3   Places correct part to ear and mouth.
4   Says 'Hello'.
5   Gives own name and/or number.
6   Asks whom caller wishes to speak to.
7   If caller wishes to speak to pupil, caller is informed that he/she is so doing.
8   Continues conversation as per objectives on 'speaking on the telephone'.
9   If caller wishes to speak to someone else, pupil asks the name of the person and indicates a willingness to fetch the person to the phone.
10 If person caller wishes to speak to is not available, pupil asks if caller wishes to leave a message.
11 Will take the message by listening, and repeat it to make sure it was heard correctly.
12 Will make note of message, or tell another adult if unable to write.

For those pupils who need maximum guidance to carry out the above objectives, a third order analysis would need to be carried out. Each of the above objectives would need to have built in a system of prompting and fading, as well as demonstrations for pupils to imitate. An example is given below:

Techniques
Modelling
Shaping
Prompting
Fading
Forward chaining

Equipment
Internal telephone system
Private telephone system

Objectives (3rd order analysis)
1   Will indicate awareness of the ringing of a telephone by looking up, by moving position or telling the teacher (according to level of ability).
2   Will move towards the telephone when it rings, with physical guidance.
3   As above with a verbal prompt.
4   Picks up receiver, with a physical prompt.
5   As above with a verbal prompt.

6   Places correct part to ear and mouth, with a physical prompt.
7   As above with a verbal prompt.
8   Will say 'Hello' and give name/number following a model.
9   As above with a physical prompt.
10   As above with a verbal prompt.
11   Asks whom caller wishes to speak to after the task has been demonstrated.
12   As above with a physical prompt.
13   As above with a verbal prompt.
14   If pupil is the one to whom the caller wishes to speak, will perform task as per objectives for 'speaking on the telephone'.
15   If caller wishes to speak to someone else, will ask to whom and indicate a willingness to fetch the person to the phone, with a physical prompt and verbal cueing.
16   As above with a verbal prompt only.
17   Where a message is to be taken, will ask for a message to be left, after following demonstration.
18   As above with a physical prompt and verbal cueing.
19   As above with a verbal prompt only.
20   Will repeat message to caller after demonstration.
21   Will do as above with a verbal prompt.
22   Will make a note of it with a physical prompt.
23   As above with a verbal prompt.

As in the programmes for the making of telephone calls, the use of a tape recorder would be an asset both for the purposes of demonstration, and to facilitate pupils' practising their skills. Where video equipment was available, pupils could be filmed once they have learned all the necessary skills for the use of the telephone, and see themselves on a replay executing a smooth skill. It could also of course be used as an aid for teachers to make assessments of the whole skill in operation immediately after the programmes have been completed, and for follow-up evaluations.

E   CROSSING A ROAD

This is a task requiring the operation of several complex skills in sequence. They include the skills of listening, recognizing crossings, and being visually alert.

Each discrete skill can be simulated in a classroom/playground before embarking on actual roads. Various pupils, or staff and pupils, can role play 'lollipop ladies', cars, buses etc. A large sheet of paper to indicate a pelican crossing with the appropriate markings can also be useful in practising these skills.

The objectives below present a sequence of steps that a pupil would have to undergo in order to achieve mastery of the skill. However, the factor of pupils having the confidence to put their skill into operation is another matter, and may well need further programming.

Objectives (3rd order analysis)

1 Will point to a pelican/pedestrian crossing in a picture.
2 As above on a model of a road.
3 As above on simulated area in playground.
4 As above on actual road.
5 Will place models of people at crossing with physical guidance, when simulating road crossing on a model.
6 As above with physical prompt.
7 As above with verbal prompt.
8 Will take model person across road on crossing on simulation exercise with physical guidance.
9 As above with physical prompt.
10 As above with verbal prompt.
11 Will stand by crossing simulated on playground when taken there, with physical guidance.
12 As above with physical prompt.
13 As above with verbal prompt.
14 Will cross on simulated crossing holding hand of adult.
15 As above following adult.
16 Will stand at simulated crossing and look left and right when teacher moves pupil's head from left to right.
17 As above with a physical prompt.
18 As above with a verbal prompt.
19 Will stand at simulated crossing and look left and right when asked to, listening for traffic noises (taped, or role played by other children).
20 Will wait for noise to pass/subside with verbal prompting before crossing on request.
21 Will stand at crossing, look right and left, and listen for traffic noise with verbal cues, and wait for cars (role played by pupils) to stop at crossing, before crossing.
22 Will cross using all above steps with one verbal prompt.

The above steps need to be repeated on an actual road before mastery can be said to have been achieved.

F   USING A BUS

The skill of using a bus involves many separate skills, for example, queuing, handling of money, asking for a particular stop, recognizing signs, bus numbers and landmarks.

Queuing can be taught for other activities, for example, shopping, and practised for getting on and off a bus. Money is covered in section C of this

chapter, while asking for stops can be taught as part of a language programme but specifically used in this context. The recognition of bus
numbers and landmarks can be taught in number recognition lessons and
social lessons. They need to be brought together for purposes of recognition
so that pupils can associate them and place them in their relevant context.

Objectives (3rd order analysis)
1 Points to a bus in a book when asked.
2 Points to a bus on a slide when asked.
3 Points to a bus on a film when asked.
4 Points to a bus on the road when asked.
5 Will point to a bus stop/shelter in a book.
6 Will point to a bus stop/shelter on a slide.
7 Will point to a bus stop/shelter on a film.
8 Will point to a bus stop/shelter on the road.
9 Will repeat name of destination after teacher.
10 Will give name of destination with a verbal clue.
11 Will give name of destination on request.
12 Will wait at simulated bus stop in playground, with physical guidance.
13 Will wait at simulated bus stop in playground, with verbal cue.
14 Will look for correct bus number placed on children's shirts (role
    playing buses).
15 Will put hand out to stop appropriately numbered bus, with physical
    guidance.
16 As above with verbal prompting.
17 As above on request.
18 Will climb steps of make believe bus holding hand of adult.
19 Will climb steps of make believe bus with physical prompt.
20 Will climb steps of make believe bus with verbal prompt.
21 Will state destination to driver/conductor after model from teacher
    (role played by pupils/staff).
22 As above with verbal prompt.
23 Will give exact money after model from adult.
24 As above with verbal prompt.
25 Will accept ticket after model from adult.
26 As above with verbal prompt.
27 Will sit in seat with physical guidance.
28 Will sit in seat with verbal prompt.
29 Will look out for specified landmark with verbal cueing from adult.
30 As above with minimal verbal cues.
31 Will make move to get up and go near door to get off, with physical
    guidance.
32 As above with verbal cues.

After simulations and role plays such as those outlined above, with pupils
taking turns to play parts of traveller, bus driver etc., the entire sequence

needs to be repeated, withdrawing the physical prompting and then the verbal prompting gradually while still role playing the exercise.

Simultaneously, games such as snap and bingo could be used to teach/reinforce signs and bus numbers. In addition the giving of fares where change is required could be introduced.

A type of backward chaining scheme can then be introduced for actual use of buses on the road, for example:

1 Will get off bus when given physical prompt.
2 As above with verbal prompt.
3 Will recognize landmark with physical cue.
4 As above with verbal cue.
5 Will sit on seat with physical prompt.
6 As above with verbal prompt.
7 Will accept ticket with verbal prompt.
8 Will give exact money with verbal prompt.
9 Will state destination with verbal prompt.
10 Will climb steps of bus with verbal prompt.
11 Will put hand out to stop bus with verbal prompt.
12 Will recognize appropriate bus with verbal prompt.
13 Will wait at bus stop with verbal prompt.

Recording the skills of independence

Children with learning difficulties vary enormously in their level of skill when it comes to the skills of independence. Depending on whether they are given adequate experiences at home, school and in the community, each child will need to be taken through a set of skills that may bear little relation to another programme operated for another pupil. For this reason, no one record sheet can establish an order to cover all the skills in this area, as that may have the effect of prejudging the sequence in which the skills are taught. Therefore it is suggested that once a skill has been selected for teaching, individual record sheets should be used to assess the rate and level of progress a pupil has made on each step of the skill. The record sheet presented on page 15 of the book should provide the necessary detail for such teaching schemes.

Once a particular area of skill has been covered, or the pupil has achieved to his or her ability, then it may be helpful for the teacher to plot this on a 'master' record sheet on Independence Skills, such as that presented on pages 154–161. In this way, it would be possible to see at a glance which skills the pupil has acquired, to what level, and how the child compares to others of his age and ability. This type of chart can also be used as illustration for parents who may wish to see for themselves what progress is being made by their child in the school setting.

Independence skills record sheet

	Date started: physical prompt	Date started: verbal prompt	Date achieved: independent
Recognition of cutlery			
Fork			
Spoon			
Knife			
Teaspoon			
Soup spoon			
Bread knife			
Vegetable knife			
Carving knife			
Random order			
Recognition and use of cooker			
Mains switch identification			
Operation of mains switch			
Bottom left hand hot plate			
Bottom right hand hot plate			
Top left hand hot plate			
Top right hand hot plate			
Grill			
Oven			
Required temperature			

	Date started: physical prompt	Date started: verbal prompt	Date achieved: independent
Recognition and use of cleaning implements			
Washing-up brush			
Sponge			
Dish cloth			
Soap pad			
Mop			
Dustpan and brush			
Pan scourer			
Duster			
Broom			
Furniture polish			
Vacuum cleaner			
Cleaning: Vacuum cleaner			
Will fetch a duster.			
Will dust furniture around objects.			
Will dust furniture removing objects and replacing items.			
Will fetch vacuum cleaner.			
Will plug in vacuum cleaner.			
Will vacuum carpet in accessible places.			
Will vaccum carpet in non-accessible places.			
Will remove plug from socket and put vacuum cleaner away.			

	Date started: physical prompt	Date started: verbal prompt	Date achieved: independent
Washing machine			
Points to washing machine.			
Switches on washing machine.			
Selects programme.			
Places clothes in machine.			
Completes operation.			
Switches off machine.			
Pegs clothes out.			
Uses tumble dryer.			
Dustpan and brush			
Grips pan and brush.			
Sweeps debris into pan.			
Puts debris into bin.			
Making snacks			
Sandwiches			
Snack on toast			
Tea			
Cold drink			
Preparing vegetables			
Household tasks: bed making			
Strips bed			
Places sheets on bed and tucks in.			

	Date started: physical prompt	Date started: verbal prompt	Date achieved: independent
Places blankets on bed and tucks in.			
Places duvet/spread.			
Places pillows near head rest.			
Care of clothes			
Folds tops.			
Folds dresses.			
Folds trousers.			
Places folded clothes in cupboard.			
Puts dirty clothes in laundry basket.			
Ironing			
Recognizes iron.			
Plugs in iron.			
Switches on iron.			
Selects suitable temperature.			
Irons cottons.			
Irons delicate materials.			
Hangs clothes on hangers.			
Telephone			
Recognizes a phone.			
Lifts receiver.			
Makes dialling movements.			
Selects correct numbers to dial.			

	Date started: physical prompt	Date started: verbal prompt	Date achieved: independent
Recalls specific phone numbers.			
Keeps a record of essential numbers.			
Speaks at appropriate time.			
Says own name.			
Waits for answers.			
Replies where necessary.			
Gives succint message.			
Waits for end of conversation to replace receiver.			
Says goodbye appropriately.			
Recognizes ringing of telephone.			
Lifts receiver and gives name.			
Takes a message.			
Relays a message.			
Calls relevant person to phone.			
Shopping: supermarket/grocer			
Will pick out and fetch six eggs.			
Will pick out and fetch pint of milk.			
Will pick out and fetch loaf of bread.			
Will pick out and fetch packet of tea.			
Will pick out and fetch jar of coffee.			
Will pick out and fetch pot of jam.			
Will pick out and fetch tin of beans.			

	Date started: physical prompt	Date started: verbal prompt	Date achieved: independent
Will pick out and fetch packet of cheese.			
Will point to shop assistant on request.			
Will ask shop assistant for item.			
Will look at assistant while asking.			
Will say please and thank you.			
Will give enough money to cover cost.			
Will wait for change.			
Will check change.			
Will put goods in bag.			
Other shops			
Points to supermarket.			
Points to newsagent's.			
Points to post office.			
Points to chemist's.			
Points to clothes shop.			
Points to shoe shop.			
Points to grocer's.			
Crossing a road			
Points to pelican crossing.			
Stands at pelican crossing to cross.			
Looks left and right.			
Listens for traffic sounds.			

	Date started: physical prompt	Date started: verbal prompt	Date achieved: independent
Waits for car to stop before crossing.			
Using a bus			
Recognizes bus.			
Recognizes bus stop.			
Requests stop.			
Boards.			
States destination.			
Gives fare.			
Waits for change.			
Accepts ticket.			
Sits on seat.			
Recognizes landmark.			
Disembarks appropriately.			
Handling money			
Points to 1p piece.			
Points to to 2p piece.			
Points to 5p piece.			
Points to 10p piece.			
Points to 20p piece.			
Points to 50p piece.			
Points to £1 note.			
Points to £5 note.			

	Date started: physical prompt	Date started: verbal prompt	Date achieved: independent
Points to £10 note.			
Adds coins to sum of 2p.			
Adds coins to sum of 3p.			
Adds coins to sum of 4p.			
Adds coins to sum of 5p.			
Adds coins to sum of 6p.			
Adds coins to sum of 7p.			
Adds coins to sum of 8p.			
Adds coins to sum of 9p.			
Adds coins to sum of 10p.			
Adds coins to sum of 12p.			
Adds coins to sum of 15p.			
Adds coins to sum of £1.			
Gives change for 10p.			
Gives change for 20p.			
Gives change for 50p.			
Gives change for £1.			

12 Token economy systems

For some older less severely handicapped pupils, the use of tokens can be effective in encourging them to use skills they have got but do not use often, or to discourage certain behaviours that are undesirable. This system has been used successfully in both classroom and residential settings (Burland *et al* 1977; Presland 1981; Neisworth & Smith 1973).

A token is a substitute or symbol of a reward that can be earned at a later date. It can take the form of stars, ticks, coloured squares, pins stuck on a chart, or pictures of objects that interest a particular child. These are symbols and they represent desirable behaviour. Other types of tokens include counters, shells, cards etc. that are more accessible to children. They can collect them and exchange them for a reward at a later date, or at specified times in the day.

The actual behaviour or behaviours that the pupil is expected to execute must be spelled out to him/her very clearly. It is not particularly helpful to tell them that they must be 'good', 'tidy' etc. without specifying what these expressions mean. It is also imperative that the pupil is made aware of where the behaviour is expected to be carried out, when, and what each behaviour is worth in terms of tokens. It is also helpful to word statements with the words 'will do ......', rather than negatively, for example, 'will not do ......'. It emphasizes that you are trying to encourage acceptable behaviours by paying more attention to them and rewarding them.

It is useful to draw up a 'menu' of rewards, each worth a different amount, so that pupils get some choice, and can save up for a particular reward. At the beginning of the operation of this system, it is best to make a popular reward reasonably attainable so as to motivate the pupil and to encourage him/her to keep on trying. As the system progresses, the rewards can be made gradually more difficult to attain, so as to ensure that the behaviours in question are well and truly in the pupil's repertoire.

The rewards must be agreed on with the pupil. They should also be changed frequently so as to avoid boredom, and to take account of particular events which may occur on a one off basis, for example, an outing. So long as it is within the pupil's grasp to attain the goal and get the reward, it is not unreasonable to use all special events and outings as rewards. In this way no child will ever be deprived of activities they should have the chance to experience, and the maximum use of resources can be made within a residential school. As each pupil will have a programme to suit all his/her needs and abilities, each will have as much chance of achieving the goals.

Token economy – Programme one: W.J. (residential setting)

W.J., a boy of thirteen, was a weekly boarder at a residential special school. He was a socially adept boy, ambulant, toilet trained, and with speech. His self-help skills were also good. He was put on an independence programme, as he was inclined to allow adults to do things for him if he was given the chance. As he was one of the more able children in the school, he was also given some tasks of responsibility to encourage his sense of self-sufficiency.

Tasks	*Tokens*
1 Making own bed	1
2 Keeping bedroom tidy	1
3 Putting clothes away	1
4 Cleaning own shoes	1
5 Putting chairs and tables away after breakfast and tea	2

W.J. was to be given one token 'star' for the first four activities, but two tokens for putting away the chairs and tables as this task proved most difficult for him to do.

Rewards	*Price*
Going to scouts	1 token
Playing on the dartboard	3 tokens
Sweets	4 tokens
Extra half hour to watch TV before bedtime	5 tokens
Going to youth club	2 tokens
Going to the park	6 tokens

Example of one week's recording: W.J.

Task	Mon.	Tues.	Wed.	Thurs.	Fri.
Making bed	x	★2 √	★2 √	√	x
Bedroom tidy	x	√	√	√	x
Clothes away	√	√	√	√	x
Cleaning shoes	√	√	√	√	x
Putting chairs and tables away	√	√	√	√	√
Reward chosen	Scouts	½ hr. extra TV	Y'th club + ½ hr. extra TV	Sweets	Darts
Number of tokens achieved	3	5	5	5	1

★These figures indicate the number of tokens earned but not spent, and
which are therefore carried over to the following day.

From the weekly recording it emerged that Friday was the worst day with
regard to W.J.'s performance, with Monday proving a poor day, but not
quite so bad. The same pattern emerged for several weeks, and it then
became evident that W.J. was due to go home on a Friday evening, and that
proved a stronger incentive than any that could be offered within the
school/hostel setting. Monday was the day that W.J. was brought for his
stint as a weekly boarder, and he would often be depressed, which would
lessen the likelihood of his performing according to plan. However, from
Tuesday to the end of the week, the rewards that he himself chose appeared
to be sufficient to motivate him to carry out the tasks assigned to him.

As soon as these factors were discovered, W.J.'s parents were consulted, and they agreed to set up suitable reinforcers for him at home during the weekend if he carried out his tasks on a Friday. However, W.J. seemed to regard going home itself as the only real reward he wanted, and although he performed slightly better on Friday and Monday, it was never as good as his performance in the rest of the week.

This case illustrates some of the limitations of a token economy system. When the reinforcers most desired by the pupil are not within the control of the staff, then it is going to be very difficult to operate the system. A decision then has to be made about what level of performance will be acceptable given that only a limited set of rewards are available for use with a particular child.

Token economy – Programme 2: A.S. (residential setting)

A.S. was a boy of almost sixteen. He had been in care since infancy, and lived in various institutions all his life. These included a children's home, a mental subnormality hospital and finally a residential special school. A.S. needed to be motivated to get out of bed in the morning and get ready for the day. He also had 'accidents' occasionally with regard to wetting. Sometimes he would give cause for concern because of his evident sexuality. Staff were somewhat afraid of allowing him to interact with pupils unsupervised. A programme whereby he was kept fully occupied during leisure hours was developed. As twenty-four hour supervision was not possible, a set of tasks, worded positively, was given to A.S. He was given tokens in the form of coloured squares, and allowed to exchange them either in the evenings or weekends.

A.S. was totally dependent on staff for all his needs and from that point of view the system was easier to operate. However, a neighbour on an estate adjoining the school befriended A.S. and visits between the two of them proved a very powerful motivator.

Tasks	Tokens
1 Getting out of bed when called	1
2 Getting washed and dressed	1
3 Taking supper trolley to kitchen in the morning	1
4 Making own bed	1
5 Keeping dry	1

A.S. had to gain a minimum of three coloured squares to be able to choose a reward from his 'menu'. This was to prevent rewards being too easily gained, especially as A.S. was likely to be included in most activities, living in the school all year round with no outside breaks. For this reason, he only earned one coloured square per activity that he successfully carried out.

A.S. therefore had to be successful three out of five times in any one day to receive the opportunity to choose a reward. An additional part of this scheme was one of withdrawal of privileges, which further helped to shape A.S.'s behaviour. This was done mainly to try and control his sexual behaviour. While he could earn rewards for getting out of bed etc., he also had to be made aware that his sexual behaviour with other children was not approved of. The 'punishments' took the form of keeping him on his own. When he interacted with others normally and not in a sexual fashion, he was rewarded for that and allowed group activities.

Rewards
1   Staying up till 9.30 p.m. on a weekday
2   Staying up till 10.00 p.m. on a weekend
3   One penny for every square coloured in
4   Visit to/from friendly neighbour
5   Going to the park

Punishments
1   Being put to bed at 8.30 p.m.
2   No scouts/youth club
3   Remaining in hostel playroom during evening activities

Example of one week's recording: A.S.

Tasks	SUNDAY	MONDAY	TUESDAY	WEDNESDAY	THURSDAY	FRIDAY	SATURDAY
Getting out of bed		✓	✓	✓	✓	✓	✓
Washing and dressing		✓	x	✓	✓	✓	✓
Taking the trolley to kitchen		✓	x	✓	✓	✓	✓
Keeping dry		✓	✓ / x	✓ / ✓	✓ / x	✓ / x	✓ / x
Making bed		✓	x	✓	x	x	x
Total		6	1	6	4	5	4
Reward		Scouts	–	Youth club	Bedtime extension	Visit neighbour	Bedtime extension
Punishment		Stay in play-room all evening					

References

AINSCOW, M. & TWEDDLE, D. A. (1979) *Preventing Classroom Failure* New York: John Wiley and Sons

AZRIN, N. H. & FOXX, R. M. (1978) *Toilet Training the Retarded* Champaign, Illinois: Research Press

BAKER, B. L., BRIGHTMAN, E. J., HEIPETZ, L. J. & MURPHY, D.N. (1978) *Steps to Independency: Basic and Intermediate Self-help Skills* (2 vols.) Barnstable: Chelfham Publications

BECKER, W. C., ENGELMANN, S. & THOMAS, D. R. (1971) *Teaching – A Course in Applied Psychology* Science Research Associates

BLAKE, K. A. (1974) *Teaching the Retarded* Englewood Cliffs, New Jersey: Prentice Hall

BLACKHAM, G. J. & SILBERMAN, A. (1975) *Modification of Child and Adolescent Behaviour* 2nd edn. Wordsworth

BRENNAN, W. K. (1974) *Shaping the Education of Slow Learners* London: Routledge & Kegan Paul

BURLAND, J. R., BROWN, T. W. & MENDHAM, R. P. (1977) *Social and Self-help Skills Training: Steps to Self Sufficiency* Chelfham Mill School: Barnstable

CLARK, D. C. (1971) 'Teaching concepts in the classroom' *Journal of Educational Psychology* 62, 253–278

DEPARTMENT OF EDUCATION AND SCIENCE (1978) *Special Educational Needs: The Warnock Report* H.M.S.O.

DEPARTMENT OF EDUCATION AND SCIENCE (1981) *Education Act 1981: Special Needs in Education* H.M.S.O.

DONALDSON, M. (1978) *Children's Minds* London: Fontana

GARDNER, W. I. (1972) *Behaviour Modification in Mental Retardation* London: University of London Press

GARDNER, J. & TWEDDLE, D. (1979) 'Some guidelines for sequencing objectives' *A.E.P. Journal* vol. 5, 2, 23–30

GRONLUND, N. E. (1978) *Stating Objectives for Classroom Instruction* 2nd edn., New York: McMillan

HARING, N. G. & BATEMAN, B. (1977) *Teaching the Learning Disabled Child* Englewood Cliffs, New Jersey: Prentice Hall

HARING, N. G. & SCHIEFLEBUSH, R. L. (eds.) (1976) *Teaching Special Children* New York: McGraw Hill

JEFFREE, D. & CHESELDINE, S. (1982) *Pathways to Independence* Sevenoaks: Hodder & Stoughton

JEFFREE, D. & McCONKEY, R. (1976) *Let Me Speak* London: Souvenir Press

KIERNAN, C. & WOODFORD, F. (eds.) (1975) *Behaviour Modification with the Severely Retarded* Associated Scientific Publishers

KIERNAN, C. & JONES, M. (1977) *Behaviour Assessment Battery* Windsor: NFER

KIERNAN, C., JORDAN, R. & SAUNDERS, C. (1978) *Starting Off* (Human Horizon Series) London: Souvenir Press

KRUMBOLTZ, J. & KRUMBOLTZ, H. (1972) *Changing Children's Behaviour* Englewood Cliffs, New Jersey: Prentice Hall

LERNER, J. W. (1976) *Children with Learning Disabilities* 2nd edn. Boston: Houghton Mifflin

MAGER, R. F. (1975) *Preparing Instructional Objectives* 2nd edn. Belmont, California: Fearnon Publishers Inc.

McKINNEY, J. D. (1973) 'Developmental study of the acquisition and utilization of conceptual strategies' *Journal of Educational Psychology* 63, 22–31

NEISWORTH, J. T. & SMITH, R. M. (1973) *Modifying Retarded Behaviour* Boston: Houghton Mifflin

POTEET, J. A. (1976) *Behaviour Modification: A Pastoral Guide for Teachers* London: University of London Press

PRESLAND, J. (1981) 'Behaviour modification in E.S.N.(S) schools' *British Psychological Society, Division of Educational and Child Psychology Occasional Papers* vol. 5, 2, 25–32

NEISWORTH, J. T. & SMITH, R. M.(1973) *Modifying retarded behaviour* Boston: Houghton Mifflin

SHIACK, G. M. (1974) *Teach them to speak* London: Ward Lock Educational

SMITH, R. M. (1974) *Clinical Teaching Methods of Instruction for the Retarded* New York: McGraw Hill

WILSON, M. (1981) *The Curriculum in Special Schools: Schools Council Programme 4* London: Schools Council

WILLIAMS, H., MUNCEY, J., WINTERINGHAM, D. & DUFFY, M. (1980) *Precision Teaching: A Classroom Manual* 2nd edn. Coventry School Psychological Service

Index

Ainscow, M. 1, 74
assessment 2, 5, 12, 16, 57, 88, 115,
    150, 153
attention
    skills 68, 70
    span 3, 13, 21, 46, 58
Azrin, N. 119

Baker, B. L. 100
Bateman, B. *see* Haring, N. G.
Becker, W. C. 87
behaviour
    control of 13–15, 162–167
    disturbed 13, 21, 87, 99, 162
    recording 13–15, 164, 167
behavioural objectives
    definition 3, 5
    orders for analysis 6–8
    sequencing of 3, 5–6, 45, 56
    value of 5
    writing of 5, 57
Blackham, G. J. 14
Blake, K. A. 1
Bliss Symbolics 7
Brennan, W. K. 1
Burland, J. R. 100, 124, 162

chaining
    backward, definition of 6–7
    exemplified in 22, 35, 37, 41–43,
        48, 83, 100, 105, 109, 115, 123,
        135, 143, 153
    forward, definition of 6–7
    exemplified in 108, 143–145, 149
charades 67–68
Cheseldine, S. *see* Jeffree, D.
children with learning difficulties
    development of 6, 57, 87
    general 5, 153
    moderate 6
    problems of 3–4, 10, 13, 65, 67,

82, 87, 100, 107
    severe 2–4, 6–7, 10, 13, 16, 46,
        57, 65, 67–68, 87, 101, 115,
        135, 137
    specific 6
Clark, D. C. 87
communication *see also* speech,
    language and vocabulary
    body posture 65–67
    body proximity 65–67
    eye contact 58, 65, 68
    facial expressions 65, 67
    non-verbal 65–68
    skills of 3, 82, 133, 141–142, 147
    systems of 45
comparison of pupils
    with other pupils 12, 53–54, 90,
        93, 98, 153
    with self 1, 5, 12, 14, 120
components
    of curriculum 3, 9
    of task 1, 3, 45, 83–84, 107, 139
concepts
    abstract 82, 85
    of colour 69, 134
    of 'different' 45, 54, 56
    of length 92
    of number 74
    of position 82
    of quantity 97, 134
    of 'same' 45, 52–54, 56
    of size 45, 88, 134
    of time 78, 82–87
    of weight 95
    understanding of 87, 93
conditions of learning 3–4
consolidation 99
criterion
    of acceptability 3
    of success 2, 13, 22, 32, 53–54,
        59–60, 71–72, 87–88, 90, 92,

95–96, 98–100, 103–105
criterion-referenced test 2
curriculum
    analysis of 3, 9
    for special needs pupils 2, 100

demonstration *see* modelling
discrimination
    auditory 87
    visual 35–36, 43, 87–88, 92, 126
Donaldson, M. 87

Education Act 1981 1
educational subnormality *see also*
        children with learning
        difficulties
    moderate 1, 3, 6
    severe 1, 3
evaluation 1, 5, 43, 50, 120, 150

fading
    definition of 8
    exemplified in 16, 22, 24, 26, 35,
        37, 41–43, 52, 100, 105, 113,
        115, 123, 136, 138, 143, 146,
        149
feedback 2, 5, 11–12, 35, 66–67, 85,
        123
fixation 4, 72
forgetting, prevention of 76, 127
Foxx, R. M. *see* Azrin, N. H.

Gardner, J. & Tweddle, D. 6
Gardner, W. I. 14
generalization 133, 135
gestures 45, 68
gratification, delay of 11
Gronlund, N. E. 5
guidance
    maximum 4, 39, 48, 144, 149
    minimum 4, 144

Haring, N. G. & Bateman, B. 1
Haring, N. G. & Schieflebush,
        R. L. 1
help *see* guidance
hyperactive 21, 101

ignoring 67
incentives 10, 111
integration of pupils
    in mainstream 1
    in the community 67, 124

Jeffree, D. & Cheseldine, S. 100, 124
Jeffree, D. & McConkey, R. 45, 63
Jones, M. *see* Kiernan, C.

Kiernan, C. & Jones, M. 16, 57, 100
Kiernan, C., Jordan, R. &
        Saunders, C. 16, 45
Kiernan, C. & Woodford, F. 14
Krumboltz, J. & Krumboltz, H. 14

language *see also* vocabulary
    appropriate/in context 61, 63, 82
    expressive 56–64
    receptive 45–56, 87
learning
    associative 10, 126
    errorless discrimination 7, 46, 50,
        52, 69, 78, 88, 92, 125, 128,
        133–134, 136
    functional 63, 126
    overlearning 69, 116
    rate of 3, 5 *see also* progress
    readiness 74
    rigidity of 4, 82
Lerner, J. W. 1

Mager, R. F. 5
mastery
    of concept 99
    of objective 6, 101, 116
    of skill, 3, 5, 108, 147, 150
    of target 3, 121
McConkey, R. *see* Jeffree, D.
McKinney, J. D. 87
measurement *see* recording
mime 67–68, 84–86
modelling
    definition of 4
    exemplified in 3, 8, 24, 26, 39–40,
        57, 59, 68, 83, 123, 125,

127–128, 130, 136, 138, 143, 146, 149
motivation
  encouraging 4, 20, 65, 110, 162, 165
  external 10, 13
  internal 10
motivators *see* reinforcement

Neisworth, J. T. & Smith, R. M. 10, 14, 162
non-verbal
  cues 37, 67, 81, 85, 144
  reinforcement 10–11, 65, 67
  responses 10
  signals 3, 58, 65, 68, 87

objectives *see* behavioural objectives
orientation 101, 107

parents *see* progress
Poteet, J. A. 14
precision teaching 43
Presland, J. 15, 162
progress
  attempts 12, 24, 26, 28, 46, 71–72, 90, 95, 101, 103, 107, 147
  erratic 5, 12, 111–113
  indicating to parents 5, 12, 153
  measuring of 13
  rate of 1, 5, 12, 46, 54, 90, 93, 98, 101, 105, 107, 118, 153
  subtle 12
  successes 12, 26, 28, 30, 43, 53–54, 61, 71–72, 90, 95, 103, 107, 111, 118
prompting, physical
  definition of 4
  exemplified in 3, 8, 16–20, 22, 24, 26, 28, 33, 39–41, 48–53, 57, 65, 75, 83–87, 100, 105, 108–110, 113–114, 120–121, 123, 125–132, 134–141, 143–146, 149–152
prompting, verbal

definition of 4
exemplified in 3, 8, 16–20, 22, 24, 26, 28, 33, 39–41, 48–53, 57, 65, 83–87, 100, 105, 108–111, 113, 115, 120–121, 123, 125–132, 134–141, 143–146, 149–152

recognition 3, 46, 69, 78, 86, 124–125, 141, 150–152
recording
  baseline 13–14, 21, 59, 105, 119–120
  consistency of 33
  examples of 14, 32, 71–72, 90, 95, 103–104, 114, 118, 164, 167
  frequency 13–14, 115, 119
  importance of 12
  progress 2, 147
  trials 13, 22, 71–72, 90, 95, 147
  types of 12
rehearsal 135
reinforcement for pupil 10, 39
  abstract 10
  attention 33, 63, 163
  concrete 10, 103–104
  continuous 20
  external 13, 43
  finding suitable 3, 10–11
  immediate 57–58, 63, 65, 68
  importance of 10
  internal 65
  physical contact 10, 20, 65, 110, 120
  praise 10, 20, 33, 65, 110, 113, 120
  timing 10–11
  tokens 11, 162–166
reinforcement for teacher 5, 12, 33
responses
  acceptable 10–11
  erratic 5, 12, 74, 111–113
  inconsistent 13
  indication of 10
  measuring of 13
  minimal 13

poor 10
unpredictable 13
rewards *see* reinforcement
role-play 66, 140–141, 150–153

Schieflebush, R. L. *see*
    Haring, N. G.
scribbling 24–25
sequencing
    auditory 82, 84
    objectives 5, 57, 88, 121
    of events 45, 56, 82, 85
    of time 83
    skills 129, 150–151
    visual 81, 83
sequential memory 82
shaping
    definition of 6
    exemplified in 10, 16, 22, 24, 26,
        28, 30, 35–37, 57, 65–68, 83,
        88, 96, 98, 115, 123, 125,
        127–128, 130, 136, 143, 146,
        149
Shiack, G. M. 45, 63
sign systems 4, 45, 48
Silberman, A. *see* Blackham, G. J.
simulation 135, 140, 150, 152
Smith, R. M. 1 *see also*
    Neisworth, J. T.
special educational needs
    literature 1
    provision 1
speech 45, 58, 61, 84, 135
    development of 57
    lack of 21, 46, 48, 70, 101
    training in 4, 57, 63
    requirements 88
steps
    grading of 2, 12, 21, 33, 46, 56,
        88, 96, 107
    moving from one to the next 2,
        12, 26, 53, 105, 107, 116
    size 5, 12, 46
stimulation 74, 88
success, chances of 3, 7
successive approximation 3, 13

symbols 46, 86, 162
systematic teaching 3, 87

tape recorder 83–85, 147, 151
task analysis
    aims 3
    complexity of 12
    concept of 2
    definition of 1
    examples of 21, 38, 48, 124
    1st order of 6, 8, 35, 45, 57,
        62–63, 65–66, 74, 136, 142,
        149
    2nd order of 6, 22, 24, 26, 28, 35
    suitability of 12, 14
    3rd order of 8, 16, 18–19, 22, 26,
        28, 33, 39–43, 46, 48–53,
        59–61, 65, 69–70, 108–109,
        120, 123, 125, 127, 129–130,
        134, 136, 138, 143–146, 149,
        151–152
teachers' comments 2, 33, 53, 61,
    72, 98
techniques of teaching 3–7 *see also*
    fading, modelling, prompting,
    shaping
    exemplified in 16, 22, 24, 26, 28,
        30, 35, 39–43, 46, 50–51, 57,
        59, 65, 68–69, 78, 83, 88, 92,
        96, 98, 100, 105, 108–109, 115,
        123, 125, 127–130, 134, 136,
        138, 143, 145–146, 149
transfer of skill 4, 136, 147
    of training 6, 82
Tweddle, D. A. *see* Ainscow, M.
    and Gardner, J.

vocabulary *see also* speech,
    communication
    expressive 56–63
    identification 48
    receptive 46, 48, 72, 87

Warnock report 1
Williams, H. 43
Wilson, M. 2, 100
Woodford, F. *see* Kiernan, C.